D0118770

THE WILD HISTORY OF THE AMERICAN WEST

THE PONY EXPRESS

AND ITS DEATH-DEFYING MAIL CARRIERS

Jeff C. Young

MyReportLinks.com Books

an imprint of

 Enslow Publishers, Inc.

Box 398, 40 Industrial Road
Berkeley Heights, NJ 07922
USA

To my uncle, Tommy Hanna

MyReportLinks.com Books, an imprint of Enslow Publishers, Inc. MyReportLinks®
is a registered trademark of Enslow Publishers, Inc.

Library of Congress Cataloging-in-Publication Data

Young, Jeff C., 1948–
  The Pony Express and its death-defying mail carriers / Jeff C. Young.
      p. cm. — (The wild history of the American West)
  Includes bibliographical references and index.
  ISBN 1-59845-010-7
  1. Pony express—History—Juvenile literature. 2. Letter carriers—United States—History—Juvenile
literature. 3. Postal service—United States—History—Juvenile literature. I. Title. II. Series.
  HE6375.P65Y68 2006
  383'.4973'09034—dc22

                                         2005018614

Printed in the United States of America

10 9 8 7 6 5 4 3 2 1

To Our Readers:
Through the purchase of this book, you and your library gain access to the Report Links that specifically
back up this book.
The Publisher will provide access to the Report Links that back up this book and will keep these Report
Links up to date on **www.myreportlinks.com** for five years from the book's first publication date.
We have done our best to make sure all Internet addresses in this book were active and appropriate when
we went to press. However, the author and the Publisher have no control over, and assume no liability
for, the material available on those Internet sites or on other Web sites they may link to.
The usage of the MyReportLinks.com Books Web site is subject to the terms and conditions stated on the
Usage Policy Statement on **www.myreportlinks.com.**
A password may be required to access the Report Links that back up this book. The password is found
on the bottom of page 4 of this book.
Any comments or suggestions can be sent by e-mail to comments@myreportlinks.com or to the address
on the back cover.

CONTENTS

MyReportLinks.com Books
Great Books, Great Links, Great for Research!

The Internet sites featured in this book can save you hours of research time. These Internet sites—we call them **"Report Links"**—are constantly changing, but we keep them up to date on our Web site.

When you see this "Approved Web Site" logo, you will know that we are directing you to a great Internet site that will help you with your research.

Give it a try! Type http://www.myreportlinks.com into your browser, click on the series title and enter the password, then click on the book title, and scroll down to the Report Links listed for this book.

The Report Links will bring you to great source documents, photographs, and illustrations. MyReportLinks.com Books save you time, feature Report Links that are kept up to date, and make report writing easier than ever! A complete listing of the Report Links can be found on pages 118–119 at the back of the book.

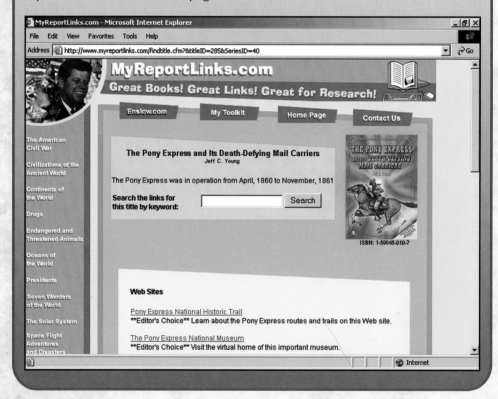

Please see "To Our Readers" on the copyright page for important information about this book, the MyReportLinks.com Web site, and the Report Links that back up this book.

Please enter **WPE1336** if asked for a password.

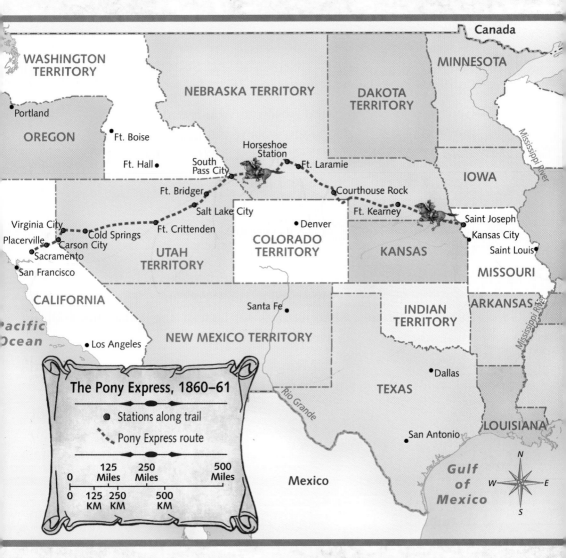

△ A map of the Pony Express route from St. Joseph, Missouri, to Sacramento, California.

▷ **1848**—*January 24:* Gold is discovered at Sutter's Mill in Coloma, California, by James Marshall.

▷ **1851**—George Chorpenning and Absolom Woodward receive a contract to move mail across the country using mules over a 700-mile route.

▷ **1854**—William H. Russell, Alexander H. Majors, and William B. Waddell create a firm to supply and outfit military posts in the West for the federal government.

▷ **1856**—Seventy-five thousand Californians petition Congress for better mail service.

▷ **1858**—*September 15:* The first of John Butterfield's coaches embarks on a 2,800-mile route to bring mail to the West Coast. The journey takes twenty-five days. Citizens and settlers in the West are still not satisfied with this service.

—Firm owned by Russell, Majors, and Waddell goes bankrupt but still has a line of credit that barely keep them in business.

▷ **1859**—William Russell meets with California Senator William Gwin to discuss establishing a ten-day mail service to California. Russell later meets with his business partners, Alexander Majors and William B. Waddell, to create the Pony Express.

▷ **1860**—*March:* The Pony Express places newspaper ads in an effort to recruit riders.

—*March 30:* First mail to be carried by the Pony Express is put on trains and delivered to St. Joseph, Missouri.

—*April 3:* The Pony Express begins operations when rider Johnny Fry leaves St. Joseph, Missouri. It has been disputed that Fry was the first rider. Some historians believe it was Johnson William Richardson.

—On the same day, a rider in San Francisco boards a steamer to Sacramento, California, to begin the first eastbound delivery.

—*April 13:* First eastern mail arrives in Sacramento.

—*May–June:* The Paiute War briefly halts service in Utah. Incident at Williams Station on May 7, triggers this clash of cultures.

—*August:* Rate for delivering a half-ounce letter drops from $5.00 to $2.50.

—*November 7:* In an attempt to drum up publicity, Pony Express promises to quickly deliver the results of the Election of 1860. The news of Lincoln's election reaches the West Coast in an amazing three days and four hours.

—*December 24:* Russell is arrested and charged with receiving stolen property and threatening to defraud the government.

▷ **1861**—Case against Russell is dismissed.

—*March:* The Pony Express makes its fastest run by delivering a copy of President Lincoln's inaugural address from St. Joseph to Sacramento in seven days and seventeen hours.

—*April:* Rate for delivering a half-ounce letter drops to $2.00.

—*July 1:* Rate for delivering a half-ounce letter drops to $1.00. Firm is losing $15.00 for every half-ounce letter they deliver.

—*October 24:* Completion of the transcontinental telegraph makes the Pony Express obsolete.

—*October 26:* Pony Express officially ceases operations.

—*November 21:* Pony Express completes its last run.

Chapter 1

"PONY BOB'S" DANGEROUS RIDE

In May 1860, the first settlers of the Utah and Nevada territories were at war with the Paiute Indians. That did not matter to a Pony Express rider known as "Pony Bob" Haslam. All that mattered to him was getting the mail delivered to his destination on time.

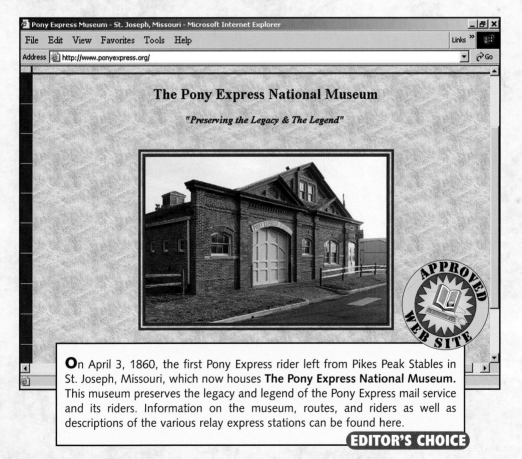

Pony Express Museum - St. Joseph, Missouri - Microsoft Internet Explorer

File   Edit   View   Favorites   Tools   Help   Links »

Address http://www.ponyexpress.org/   Go

The Pony Express National Museum

"Preserving the Legacy & The Legend"

On April 3, 1860, the first Pony Express rider left from Pikes Peak Stables in St. Joseph, Missouri, which now houses **The Pony Express National Museum.** This museum preserves the legacy and legend of the Pony Express mail service and its riders. Information on the museum, routes, and riders as well as descriptions of the various relay express stations can be found here.

EDITOR'S CHOICE

The Paiute believed that the settlers of the territories that would later become the states Utah and Nevada had invaded their homeland. The settlers believed that they had a right to take the land and make it their own. The Paiute responded to what they felt was an intrusion on their land by stealing horses, burning houses, and killing settlers.

On May 9, Haslam was at a Pony Express station on the California-Nevada border known as Friday's Station. Haslam was anxious and worried. The rider he was replacing was running late. The stationmaster speculated that some Paiute warriors may have ambushed the tardy rider, but Haslam thought otherwise.

Finally, Haslam saw a cloud of dust on the distant horizon. He was certain it was his fellow rider, Tom King. King rode in, quickly dismounted, and passed the leather *mochila* to Haslam. A mochila is the leather sack that the Pony Express riders used to carry the mail. "Pony Bob" threw the mochila over his saddle and rapidly rode away.

The ride started off. Haslam changed horses twice before reaching Reed's Station on or ahead of schedule. But when he arrived at Reed's Station, there was no replacement horse waiting for him. All the available horses had been seized by volunteer soldiers to help fight the Paiute.

Haslam would later recall, "When I reached Reed's Station on the Carson River, I found no

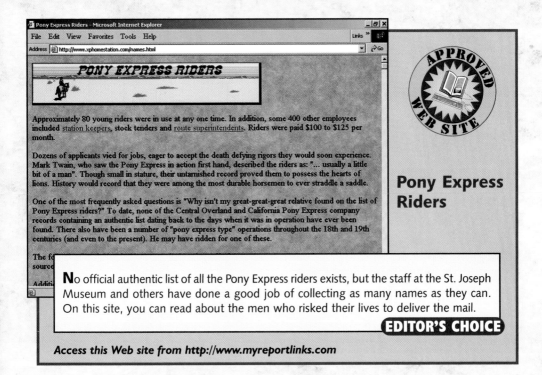

PONY EXPRESS RIDERS

Approximately 80 young riders were in use at any one time. In addition, some 400 other employees included station keepers, stock tenders and route superintendents. Riders were paid $100 to $125 per month.

Dozens of applicants vied for jobs, eager to accept the death defying rigors they would soon experience. Mark Twain, who saw the Pony Express in action first hand, described the riders as: "... usually a little bit of a man". Though small in stature, their untarnished record proved them to possess the hearts of lions. History would record that they were among the most durable horsemen to ever straddle a saddle.

One of the most frequently asked questions is "Why isn't my great-great-great relative found on the list of Pony Express riders?" To date, none of the Central Overland and California Pony Express company records containing an authentic list dating back to the days when it was in operation have ever been found. There also have been a number of "pony express type" operations throughout the 18th and 19th centuries (and even to the present). He may have ridden for one of these.

Pony Express Riders

No official authentic list of all the Pony Express riders exists, but the staff at the St. Joseph Museum and others have done a good job of collecting as many names as they can. On this site, you can read about the men who risked their lives to deliver the mail.

EDITOR'S CHOICE

Access this Web site from http://www.myreportlinks.com

change of horses, as all those at the station had been seized by the whites to take part in the approaching battle. I fed the animal that I rode and started for the next station."[1]

Bob Haslam rode his weary horse along the Carson River to Buckland's Station. He had ridden the tired mount nearly eighty miles. Buckland's was supposed to be the end of his route. However, when Haslam got there, there was no relief rider waiting outside for him.

Haslam entered the station and found the stationmaster, W. C. Marley, and the relief rider, Johnson Richardson, idly playing cards. Richardson claimed that he was too sick to ride. Marley said that Richardson was making excuses because he was afraid of being attacked by the Paiute. This was the only recorded instance of a Pony Express rider refusing to make a run.

The two men, Haslam and Marley, tried to persuade Richardson to take the mochila and ride his route. Richardson stubbornly refused to leave the safety of the station, so Marley made Haslam a solid offer.

"Bob, I will give you fifty dollars to make this ride," Marley said.[2]

"I will go at once," Bob replied.[3]

After arming himself with a seven-shot Spencer rifle and a Colt revolver, Haslam threw the mochila over the saddle of a fresh horse. He rode another 35 miles to the Sink of the Carson Station. Carson Sink is a lake in what is now western Nevada. He quickly changed horses there.

Even with a fresh horse, Haslam still had about another ninety miles of hard riding ahead of him. He had to ride across 30 miles of sand hills and over alkali bottoms without anything to drink. Pony Bob Haslam blocked out his fatigue, aching muscles, and parched throat and gamely rode on.

At the Sand Springs Station, Haslam changed horses again and probably took a few seconds to quench his thirst. Somewhere between the Sand Springs and Cold Springs stations, Haslam was attacked by some warring Paiutes. He crouched down further in the saddle to avoid their flying arrows and bullets.

Bob Haslam had a speedy horse, but he could not outrun his attackers. That puzzled him, until he remembered that the Paiute had recently raided some of the Pony Express relay stations. The Paiutes were chasing Haslam on Pony Express horses.

Haslam returned their fire and shot one of the Paiutes off of his horse. The other warriors maintained their pursuit. Then, Haslam felt a sharp burning pain surging through his shoulder. He

http://memory.loc.gov/afc/afc96ran/440/44086v.jpg - Microsoft Internet Explorer

File   Edit   View   Favorites   Tools   Help   Links »

Address http://memory.loc.gov/afc/afc96ran/440/44086v.jpg   ⌄ 🔗Go

Done

The terrain in Paradise Valley, Nevada, shown here at this Library of Congress Web site named **The Pony Express**, is very similar to sections of the route taken by Pony Express riders.

was shot! One arm dropped limply to his side. Moments later, a second bullet grazed his cheek.

Haslam rode on at full gallop until the shooting stopped. He looked over his shoulder to find that his attackers had given up. He rode into the Cold Springs Station bloodied and fatigued, but he was still determined to finish his route.

△ A photograph of Pony Express rider Frank E. Webner, taken around 1861.

When the station keeper saw Bob, he said: "You're in no shape to ride, Bill or me will take the mochila on."[4]

Pony Bob Haslam flatly refused. "Get me a horse," Haslam ordered. "I'm going through."[5]

Haslam dressed his wound by wrapping a towel around his shoulder. He rode on to the Smith's Creek Station and handed the mochila over to his relief rider, J. G. Kelley.

That is when Haslam's ride should have ended. He finally got some sleep. Most accounts say that he rested for eight or nine hours before the station keeper awakened him.

There was some bad news. The westbound rider had broken his leg after being thrown from his horse. The station keeper asked if Bob would saddle up again and make the westbound run back to Friday's Station.

Bob Haslam quickly said yes.

"He (the injured rider) stays, but not the mochila," Haslam said. "That mail's got to go through. I'm riding!"[6]

When he got to the Cold Springs Station, Bob found that Paiute Indians had burned down the station, killed the station keeper, and stolen all the horses. So, Bob Haslam quickly decided to keep riding.

"I watered my horse," he recalled. "Having ridden him thirty miles on time he was pretty tired

. . . It was growing dark and my road laid through heavy sagebrush, high enough in some places to conceal a horse. I kept a bright lookout and closely watched every motion of my poor pony's ears, which is a signal for danger in Indian country."[7]

With the howls of wolves echoing in his ears, Haslam rode on to the Sand Springs Station. Upon arriving there, he told the stationmaster about the attack on the Cold Springs Station. He warned him of impending danger and convinced him to ride along with him.

Haslam pressed on to Carson Sink, Buckland's, and finally on to Friday's Station. "I had traveled 380 miles within a few miles of schedule time and was surrounded by perils on every hand," he later recalled.[8]

For his courage, determination, and devotion to duty, the Pony Express gave Pony Bob Haslam a fifty-dollar bonus. He was happy to get it, but he did not consider himself a hero. He felt that he was just doing his job.

Chapter 2

MAIL ROUTES TO THE WEST

The biggest gold rush in American history helped lead to the founding of the Pony Express. In 1848, gold was discovered at Sutter's Mill, located just east of Sacramento, California. By the end of that year, four thousand prospectors were panning California's American River for gold. A year later, another eighty thousand gold seekers, known as forty-niners, had flooded into California hoping to strike it rich. By 1852, over two hundred thousand prospectors had crowded into a narrow 150-square-mile area of rich gold deposits in the western foothills of the Sierra Nevada Mountains.

▷ Getting News to Western Settlers

Along with their lust for gold and dreams of sudden wealth, the prospectors brought with them a thirst for news from home and the outside world. At that time, mail service was slow, erratic, and undependable. There were no railroads west of the Missouri River, so the mail traveled by steamship and on the wooden wheels of stagecoaches.

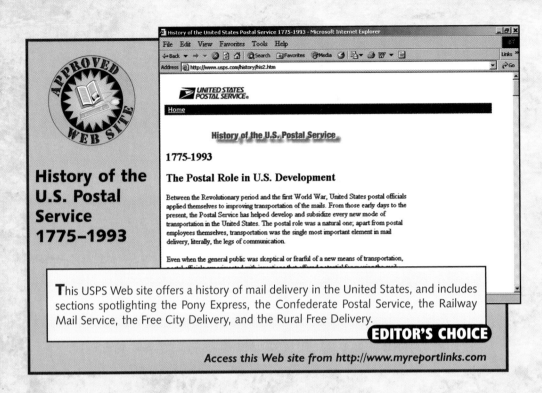

History of the U.S. Postal Service 1775–1993

History of the United States Postal Service 1775-1993 - Microsoft Internet Explorer

File   Edit   View   Favorites   Tools   Help

Back   →   ⊗ ⊠ ⌂ | ⊗Search ⊞Favorites ⊛Media ⊗ | ⊠▾ ⊜ ⊠ ▾ ⊠

Address ⊠ http://www.usps.com/history/his2.htm   ⊠ ⊘Go

UNITED STATES POSTAL SERVICE®

Home

History of the U.S. Postal Service

1775-1993

The Postal Role in U.S. Development

Between the Revolutionary period and the first World War, United States postal officials applied themselves to improving transportation of the mails. From those early days to the present, the Postal Service has helped develop and subsidize every new mode of transportation in the United States. The postal role was a natural one; apart from postal employees themselves, transportation was the single most important element in mail delivery, literally, the legs of communication.

Even when the general public was skeptical or fearful of a new means of transportation,

This USPS Web site offers a history of mail delivery in the United States, and includes sections spotlighting the Pony Express, the Confederate Postal Service, the Railway Mail Service, the Free City Delivery, and the Rural Free Delivery.

EDITOR'S CHOICE

Access this Web site from http://www.myreportlinks.com

A handmade wooden sign at the general store in a gold-mining town called Poverty Slope summed up the state of mail service. It said, "Gold is Where You Find it. Mail is when you Get it." Depending on the weather, it would take from three to six weeks for a letter to travel from New York to California. There was no direct route connecting America's East and West Coasts.

A steamship would travel down the eastern seaboard to the Isthmus of Panama in Central America. This is prior to the existence of the Panama Canal, which was not completed until 1914. Then, the mail would be hauled overland by rail and horseback to the Pacific coast of Panama.

Another steamship would then haul the mail from Panama to San Francisco, California.

Chorpenning and Woodward

One early attempt to improve mail service after the California Gold Rush came in 1851. The United States government solicited bids for delivering mail between Sacramento, California, and Salt Lake City, Utah. George Chorpenning and Absolom Woodward were the low bidders with a bid of fourteen thousand dollars.

They used mules to move the mail along the 700-mile route. The contract called for them to complete the route in thirty days. The enterprise was a failure. American Indian attacks, deep

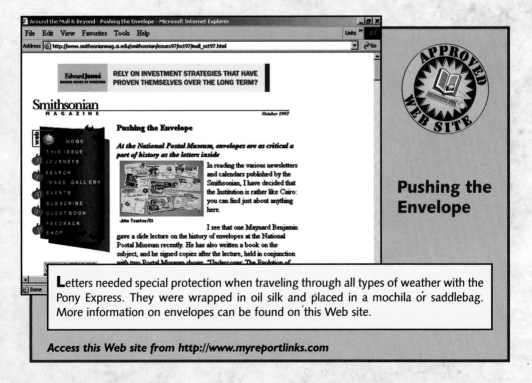

Pushing the Envelope

Letters needed special protection when traveling through all types of weather with the Pony Express. They were wrapped in oil silk and placed in a mochila or saddlebag. More information on envelopes can be found on this Web site.

Access this Web site from http://www.myreportlinks.com

snowdrifts, and freezing temperatures delayed or halted the mail. Woodward was killed in an American Indian attack. When the mail did get through, it took about fifty-four days to complete the route.

Using Camels and Dogs

For a brief time, camels were used to haul mail from Texas to California. Since they were desert creatures with great endurance, the idea seemed feasible.

▲ Freight companies even tried using camels, like those pictured here, to carry goods in the 1800s. These particular animals are in their native Africa.

Mail carriers soon found that camels were unsuitable for traveling across the rocky deserts of southwestern America. Their hooves were accustomed to soft desert sand. They tried covering the camel's hooves with leather boots, but that slowed the animals down too much.

It was also discovered that other animals used for transporting mail and freight—mules, oxen, and horses—became frightened and confused when they were around camels. A mere whiff of a camel would rile up the usually calm beasts of burden and make them unruly. The experiment ended after only one trip. The camels were retired as mail carriers and sold off to circuses.

Other Strange Ideas

Another unusual method of moving mail at that time and place was the use of skiers and dogsleds. A mail carrier named John "Snowshoe" Thompson used 10-foot, cross-country skis to move the mail about 90 miles from Placerville, California, to Genoa, Nevada. Thompson made the trip in just three days. The drawback, of course, was that this method of travel could only be used in areas where it snowed frequently.

Despite the best efforts of man, machine, and beasts of burden, transcontinental mail service in the 1850s was still slow, erratic, and unreliable.

While there was a strong interest in linking the East and West coasts with a transcontinental railroad, sectional politics stalled the project. Southern politicians wanted the railroad to go through their area. Northern politicians wanted a northern route for linking the two coasts.

Congress Steps In

In the meantime, residents of the western states and territories were becoming increasingly frustrated and impatient with the quality of the mail service. In 1856, Congress was presented with a petition signed by seventy-five thousand Californians, who demanded improved overland mail service. One year later, Congress responded by passing a bill authorizing a transcontinental mail service to compete with the New York to Panama to San Francisco mail carriers.

The bill set down conditions that had to be met. The mail service would be provided by "good four-horse coaches or spring wagons suitable for the conveyance of passengers, as well as the safety and security of the mail."[1] The bill also ordered that the route would be from a specified point of the Mississippi River to San Francisco, California. Land would be provided for rest stations, and each trip would have to be completed in twenty-five days or less. After advertising for bidders, the Post Office Department received bids from nine

This portrait of President James Buchanan was painted by an artist at the firm N. Currier, modeled after a portrait taken by photographer Matthew Brady. Buchanan's postmaster general had to create a mail route that avoided Utah because of the ongoing problems between the federal government and the people then known as the Mormons.

contractors. The bidders proposed several different routes.

▷ Different Ideas

One bidder proposed a northern route that began in St. Paul, Minnesota. Two bidders favored a central route going through Salt Lake City, Utah. Four bidders proposed southern routes starting in either St. Louis, Missouri, or Memphis, Tennessee, and then going through New Mexico, Arizona, and southern California. Two bidders did not even offer details of a specific route they might use.

Northerners expected that the preferred route would be the well-traveled one going through Salt Lake City. This route was known as the Mormon

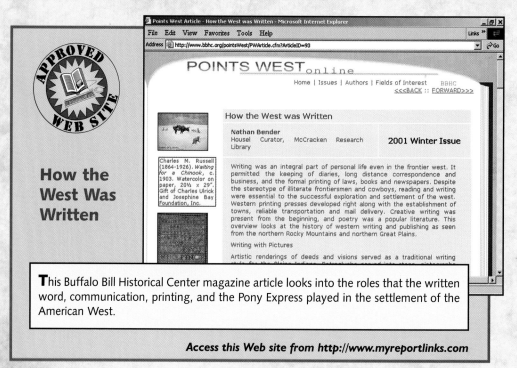

How the West Was Written

This Buffalo Bill Historical Center magazine article looks into the roles that the written word, communication, printing, and the Pony Express played in the settlement of the American West.

Access this Web site from http://www.myreportlinks.com

Trail and had brought settlers west for decades. The final decision would be made by the postmaster general, Aaron W. Brown.

Before joining the Cabinet of President James Buchanan, Brown had served as governor of Tennessee. Since he was a southerner, Brown preferred a southern route. He angered and disappointed northerners by picking a route none of the bidders had proposed.

In the route Brown chose, mail and passengers would depart from both Memphis and St. Louis to converge in Little Rock, Arkansas. From Little Rock, they would travel westward through Texas and what are now New Mexico and Arizona, and then along a yet-to-be-built road in California.

Problems in Utah

Brown may have wanted to avoid the central route through Utah because the United States was technically at war with the Mormon Church, now known as The Church of Jesus Christ of Latter-day Saints.

In 1857, President Buchanan sent a 2,500-man military force into Utah to oust Mormon leader Brigham Young from his post as governor of the Utah Territory. Buchanan was a Democrat, and Republicans charged that by allowing Young to remain in power, the president favored the "Twin relics of barbarism, polygamy and slavery."[2]

△ Brigham Young, shown here, was the leader of the Mormon people. The Mormon church is officially known as The Church of Jesus Christ of Latter-day Saints.

Buchanan believed that replacing Young with a non-Mormon governor would quiet these charges. In fact, many people disapproved of the Mormons because they practiced polygamy—allowing a man to have more than one wife.

Young responded to the show of force by declaring martial law and using the local militia to harass and delay the invading troops. The Mormon militia burned three supply trains and drove away hundreds of government cattle.

The so-called war ended in June 1858 after Young vacated the governorship and allowed the U.S. Army to establish a garrison in the Utah Territory. In return, Buchanan issued a blanket pardon to all the Mormons who burned the trains and drove away the cattle.

Butterfield's Bid

The winning bid for using the southern route was submitted by John Butterfield.

Butterfield agreed to deliver mail and transport passengers on a semiweekly schedule for six hundred thousand dollars a year. Butterfield was backed by the four major express delivery companies of that time—Adams, American, National, and Wells Fargo.

The southern route was 760 miles longer than the northern one, but it avoided crossing the Sierra Nevada Mountains and the harsh subzero winters and blizzards of the northern plains. What it did not avoid, however, was hostile American Indians. Comanche and Apache roamed the Southwest and would regard the stagecoaches as intruders on their lands.

Butterfield put his plan into action by hiring eight hundred men to build stagecoach stations every 20 miles along the route. He also bought one hundred new coaches and manned the stations with stock tenders and keepers. Butterfield also purchased additional horses, harnesses, tools, and equipment. It is estimated that he spent around one million dollars to fulfill the terms of a six-hundred-thousand-dollar contract.

Hazards of the Southern Route

On September 15, 1858, the first of Butterfield's coaches left St. Louis for the West Coast. Also that day, a second coach departed San Francisco to go east. Butterfield was contracted to deliver the mail along a 2,800-mile route in only 25 days. That required the coaches to average 112 miles a day in all kinds of weather.

Along with the uncertain weather and road conditions, the routes the coaches followed were plagued by attacks from hostile American Indians. Apache, Kiowa, and Comanche warriors would burn the coaches, kill the passengers, and discard the undelivered mail.

▲ At the time the Pony Express was created, the stagecoach was the most popular way to carry mail and freight to the West. This night-scene painting is "The Old Stage Coach of the Plains" by Frederic Remington.

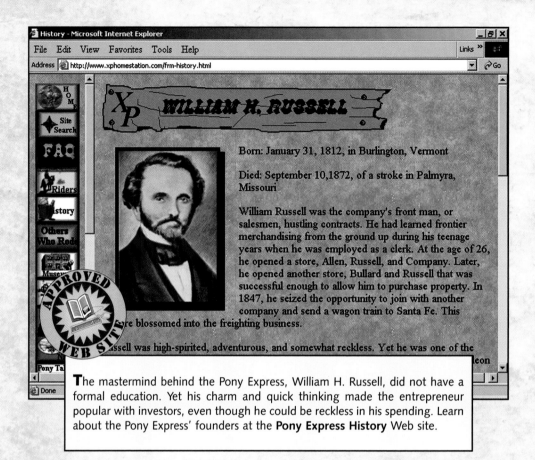

History - Microsoft Internet Explorer

File   Edit   View   Favorites   Tools   Help   Links »

Address   http://www.xphomestation.com/frm-history.html   Go

H
O
M

Site
Search

FAQ

Riders

History

Others
Who Rod

Museu

APPROVED

WEB SITE

Pony Ta

Done

WILLIAM H. RUSSELL

Born: January 31, 1812, in Burlington, Vermont

Died: September 10,1872, of a stroke in Palmyra, Missouri

William Russell was the company's front man, or salesmen, hustling contracts. He had learned frontier merchandising from the ground up during his teenage years when he was employed as a clerk. At the age of 26, he opened a store, Allen, Russell, and Company. Later, he opened another store, Bullard and Russell that was successful enough to allow him to purchase property. In 1847, he seized the opportunity to join with another company and send a wagon train to Santa Fe. This ...re blossomed into the freighting business.

...ssell was high-spirited, adventurous, and somewhat reckless. Yet he was one of the ...leon

The mastermind behind the Pony Express, William H. Russell, did not have a formal education. Yet his charm and quick thinking made the entrepreneur popular with investors, even though he could be reckless in his spending. Learn about the Pony Express' founders at the **Pony Express History** Web site.

▷ Still Too Slow

Even when the twenty-five-day deadline was met, people were still not entirely satisfied. Senator William M. Gwin of California began lobbying for a shorter northern route to replace the southern route. He could not find much support from his fellow senators. President Buchanan and Postmaster General Brown stood by their decision to continue to use the southern route.

However, Senator Gwin's efforts did not go completely unnoticed. William H. Russell of the freighting firm of Russell, Majors, and Waddell traveled to Washington, D.C., to see the senator. Russell had an idea that seemed absurd. He would use a relay team of horses and riders to move the mail from east to west in only ten days.

Chapter 3 ▶

STARTING UP THE BUSINESS

The three men who founded and bankrolled the Pony Express—William H. Russell, Alexander H. Majors, and William B. Waddell—were wealthy and successful businessmen when the enterprise began. When it ended, they were financially ruined.

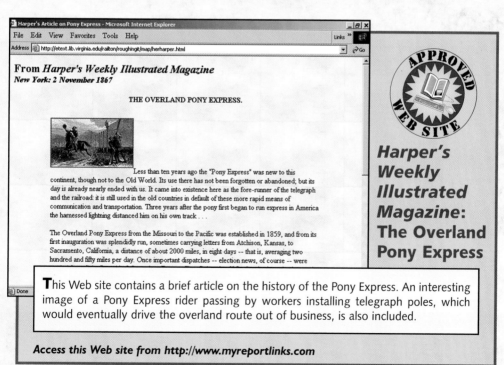

Harper's Weekly Illustrated Magazine: The Overland Pony Express

This Web site contains a brief article on the history of the Pony Express. An interesting image of a Pony Express rider passing by workers installing telegraph poles, which would eventually drive the overland route out of business, is also included.

Access this Web site from http://www.myreportlinks.com

Successful Businessmen

Russell and Majors had earned their fortunes in the freighting business. They owned dozens and dozens of wagons used for hauling people and goods across America. Their wagons traveled to practically every town, frontier settlement, and mining camp.

In 1858, noted newspaper editor Horace Greeley saw the firm's depot in Leavenworth, Kansas, and wrote:

Such acres of wagons! Such pyramids of extra axles! Such herds of oxen! Such regiments of drivers and other employees! No one who does not see can realize how vast a business this can be, and how immense are its outlays as well as its income. I presume that this great firm has at this hour two million dollars invested in stock, mainly oxen, mules and wagons. They last year employed six thousand teamsters and worked forty-five thousand oxen.[1]

William Waddell worked as a lead miner, a store clerk, a farmer, and then as a dry goods merchant before forming a business partnership with Russell. In 1853, they formed a large retail and wholesale trading firm based in Lexington, Kentucky. That same year, they used a wagon train to haul military supplies to army forts in Kansas and New Mexico.

The Partnership

By 1854, the federal government began looking for a more efficient way to outfit and supply the military posts west of the Missouri River. Instead of hiring numerous small outfits, they decided to use one large firm to supply most of the military outposts. A two-year contract went up for competitive bidding. That led Russell, Majors, and Waddell to form a partnership. They realized that they could not compete individually, but pooling their freighting experience, skills, money, and talents would make them competitive.

Each of the partners had a clearly defined role in the organization. Russell traveled to New York, Philadelphia, and Washington, D.C., seeking contracts from government officials and business capital from banks. Waddell supervised the everyday operations and dealings with local officials to ensure that things ran smoothly. Majors was in charge of freighting operations. He hired the teamsters, loaded the wagon trains, and saw to it that they ran on schedule.

Money Coming In

Only three months after its formation, the firm of Russell, Majors, and Waddell got its first government contract. The U.S. Department of War awarded them a two-year contract for supplying military stores between Fort Union, New Mexico,

In order to start an express service, investors needed money to buy start-up materials and hire workers such as relay stationkeepers and blacksmiths. This blacksmith is forging horseshoes for animals that will be following the old route of the Pony Express.

and Salt Lake City, Utah. The new firm quickly learned and developed organizational and management skills.

Starting up a freighting business required a lot of money for building, as well as hiring the workforce. Bunkhouses, warehouses, corrals, stables, and blacksmith shops all had to be built from the ground up. Workers would be needed to manage and maintain the properties. Even more workers were needed to handle the freight and keep the wagons moving on schedule. They all had to be recruited, hired, and transported to their work site.

Dissension in the Ranks

Russell, Majors, and Waddell usually got along. Even still, there were some conflicts because of personality differences. One historian described their differences by writing:

> Both Majors and Waddell leaned decidedly to the conservative side of things. Russell was exactly the opposite. He was quick to make decisions, bold in carrying them out, and implicitly believed that every enterprise with which he was connected would turn out to be a bonanza. Majors and Waddell were deliberate, conservative, slow to make decisions, and unwilling to take long chances."[2]

The major conflicts were between Russell and Waddell. Waddell did not like how much time Russell was spending back east. He also questioned

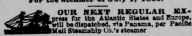

Expresses.

WELLS, FARGO & CO.'S
Express Notice.

For the Steamer of July 1, 1861.

OUR NEXT REGULAR EX-
press for the Atlantic States and Europe,
will be dispatched, via Panama, per Pacific
Mail Steamship Co.'s steamer

ST. LOUIS,

W. F. LAPIDGE............... COMMANDER,

ON MONDAY............ ....JULY 1,

AT 9 O'CLOCK, A. M.

TREASURE shipped at Reduced Rates, and INSURED under
our own policies held with the best English Companies, viz :
   Indemnity Mutual Insurance Company ;
   Marine Insurance Company ;
   Royal Exchange Insurance Company ; and
   London Assurance Company.
Treasure received for shipment until 12 o'clock on the night
previous to the sailing of the steamer ; and small packages and
parcels received until within one hour of the time of sailing.
EXCHANGE drawn on most of the principal cities and towns
in the Atlantic States.
                WELLS, FARGO & CO.,
je27   Parrott's Building, Montgomery street.

Pony Express Notice,

....FOR THE....

Service Commencing, July 1, 1861.

PLACERVILLE TO ST. JOSEPH.

THE OVERLAND MAIL COMPANY'S
"PONY EXPRESS" will be dispatched regularly FROM
THE OFFICE OF THEIR AGENCY, AT PLACERVILLE,
On the Arrival of the
EXPRESS LEAVING SAN FRANCISCO
Wednesday and Saturday
OF EACH WEEK.
ALL LETTERS must be enclosed in ten-cent Government
Stamped Envelopes and prepaid, at the rate of one dollar for each
half-ounce or any fraction thereof.
MESSRS. WELLS, FARGO & CO. HAVE
BEEN APPOINTED AGENTS, and letters will be received
and delivered at their offices.
           WILLIAM BUCKLEY,
je26-tf   Superintendent O. M. Co.

Pony Express Notice,

...... FOR THE ......

Service Commencing July 1, 1861.

MESSRS. WELLS, FARGO & CO.

WILL RUN A

Pony Express

....BETWEEN...

SAN FRANCISCO AND PLACERVILLE,

Regularly on

Wednesday and Saturday,

OF EACH WEEK,

Leaving their office at 3:45 P. M., on these days, and
Connecting with the Overland Mail Company's
Pony Express at Placerville.
LETTERS MUST BE ENCLOSED IN OUR TWENTY-
CENT GOVERNMENT FRANKED ENVELOPES, and
Charges FROM PLACERVILLE PREPAID AT THE RATE
OF ONE DOLLAR FOR EACH HALF-OUNCE, OR ANY
FRACTION THEREOF.
  All letters not enclosed as above will be charged at the
rate of 25 cents each.
je26-tf   WELLS, FARGO & CO.

These notices for express services, including the Pony Express, appeared in a newspaper in 1861.

some of Russell's expenditures and decisions. Russell was known to neglect important details and ignore requests from Waddell for instructions.

In spite of their differences, their new firm prospered during its first two years. In his memoirs, Majors writes that the firm had a profit of $300,000 from its first government contract.

▷ Helping the Government Lost Them Money

In February 1857, the firm signed its second contract with the War Department. But instead of increased profits, the second contract led to eventual bankruptcy. The outbreak of the Utah War in May 1857 required a great increase in shipments of military freight. The deployment of twenty-five hundred troops to march on Utah required the firm to add enough wagons ". . . to transport two and a half to three million tons of military freight."[3]

During the Utah War, the firm lost several wagon trains of provisions along with equipment and oxen. The War Department never paid Russell, Majors, and Waddell for their losses.

To fulfill the contract and cover their losses, Russell convinced Secretary of War John B. Floyd to solicit funds for his firm. Secretary Floyd wrote letters to various financiers and bankers asking them to loan money to Russell, Majors, and Waddell. The loans would be repaid from antici- pated earnings the firm would get from an 1858 military freighting contract. From October 1858 to March 1860, the freighting firm received over $5 million in loans.

According to one historian, the firm of Russell, Majors, and Waddell went bankrupt during the winter of 1857–58. Still, they had a line of credit. They hoped that the Pony Express would be their financial salvation. The risks were great, but so were the rewards. A big overland government mail contract would save the firm.

▶ A New Idea

Just exactly who first thought of using a system of horses and relay stations for moving the mail

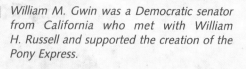

William M. Gwin was a Democratic senator from California who met with William H. Russell and supported the creation of the Pony Express.

across the continent is not clear. Alexander Majors was the only one of the firm's founders to write an autobiography. According to Majors, the idea for the Pony Express originated in 1859 during meetings between Russell and California Senator William Gwin. Gwin was then chairman of the Senate Post Office and Post Roads Committee. Majors claims that Gwin asked Russell to come up with a central route for delivering the mail.

At that time, the most widely used routes were the Southern Route, used by Butterfield, and the Oxbow Route, which meandered from Missouri to El Paso, Texas, and then ran through the Southwestern United States before ending in California.

The shortest distance between two points is a straight line. In this case, the straight line would be from the Missouri River to the California coast. Gwin asked Russell to start up an experimental mail service using horses. The freighting firm was already running a stage line from the Missouri River to Salt Lake City. Gwin wanted them to extend the route westward from Salt Lake City to Sacramento.

Gwin could not give any firm assurances of a government contract to subsidize the operation. First they had to prove that it could be done. That meant showing they could cross both the Rocky Mountain and Sierra Nevada ranges in the worst winter weather. It also meant crossing hundreds of miles of desert and lands occupied by potentially hostile American Indians.

▷ A Risky Endeavor

All Gwin could offer in return was a promise to use his influence to get them a government mail contract. That was good enough for Russell, but Majors and Waddell were understandably skeptical. Majors bluntly told his partners the enterprise would never be profitable. Russell reportedly threatened to go it alone if his partners backed out. His bluff worked, and Majors and Waddell reluctantly went along.

Russell had boldly promised Gwin that the new mail service would be up and running in sixty-five days. The route Russell proposed was 1,966 miles long and would run through eight states and territories. A total of 138 relay stations would have to be built, maintained, and staffed. The best horses

Map of the Pony Express Route

The Pony Express riders traveled from St. Joseph, Missouri, to Sacramento, California, dropping mail off as they rode along the route. View an old map of the route made available by the Union Pacific Railroad.

EDITOR'S CHOICE

Access this Web site from http://www.myreportlinks.com

would be bought and the best riders would be recruited and hired.

Buying Supplies

The firm paid top dollar for horses with exceptional speed and endurance. In case of attacks by American Indians, the riders would have to flee instead of fight. Thoroughbreds from Kentucky were the horse of choice for crossing the flat terrain of open prairies. Hardy mustangs were used for the western foothills and mountain ranges. Pintos and Morgans were also purchased.

The usual price for a saddle horse was $50, but the Pony Express paid from $150 to $200. In

March 1860, they placed an ad in the *Weekly West* and other newspapers that read:

WANTED: TWO HUNDRED GRAY MARES WITH black hoofs, not more than fifteen hands high, to carry the mails. Apply to Russell, Majors & Waddell, Central Overland, California, and Pike's Peak Express Company.[4]

Still, not all of the horses they used were thoroughbreds and pedigrees. According to some sources, half-wild horses were also used. One far-rier (a person who shoes horses) working for the Pony Express claimed that it took three men to shoe one of the half-wild horses. After tying a rope around each leg, one man would hold the horse's head and another would mount the horse. Then, it

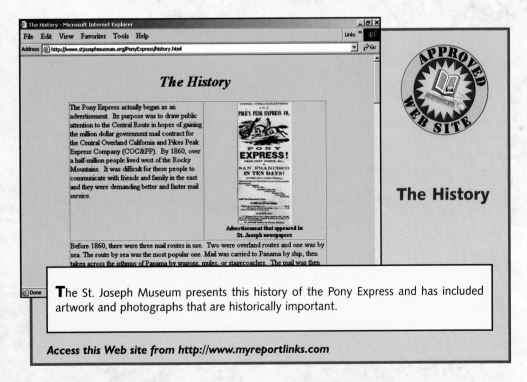

The St. Joseph Museum presents this history of the Pony Express and has included artwork and photographs that are historically important.

Access this Web site from http://www.myreportlinks.com

would still take the farrier about half a day to shoe the horse.

Pete Neece, who broke horses for the Pony Express, claimed that a horse was considered to be broken: "when a rider could lead it out of the stable without getting his head kicked off."[5]

Even the swiftest and most obedient horses were useless without able, adept, and experienced riders. After buying, breaking, and outfitting around five hundred horses, the Pony Express began recruiting riders. It is estimated that four hundred or five hundred men applied to be riders, but only eighty were chosen.

Riders Wanted

In March 1860, a now famous ad was placed in several newspapers:

> WANTED—young, skinny wiry fellows, not over eighteen. Must be expert riders willing to risk death daily. Orphans preferred. Wages $25 a week. Apply Central Overland Express, Alta Bldg., Montgomery St.

Russell had a certain kind of rider in mind. The riders had to weigh less than 125 pounds. Drinkers and reckless, foolhardy adventurers were eliminated. They had to be fearless and of good character. The preferred age was twenty, but many of the riders were in their teens. According to Pony Express legend, the youngest rider, Bronco Charlie

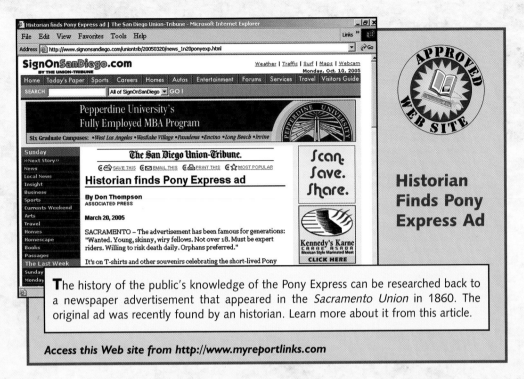

The history of the public's knowledge of the Pony Express can be researched back to a newspaper advertisement that appeared in the *Sacramento Union* in 1860. The original ad was recently found by an historian. Learn more about it from this article.

Access this Web site from http://www.myreportlinks.com

Miller, was only eleven when he rode for the Pony Express. The oldest riders were believed to be in their mid-forties.

Although the riders were chosen hastily, they were carefully screened. Anyone who weighed too much was eliminated. After being hired, each rider was given a Bible and then took an oath saying he would not fight, swear, or abuse his horse. Along with honoring that pledge, riders were expected to always obey an unwritten rule: MAIL FIRST: HORSE SECOND: SELF LAST.

Relay Stations

Along with hiring horses and riders, a series of relay stations had to be quickly built along the

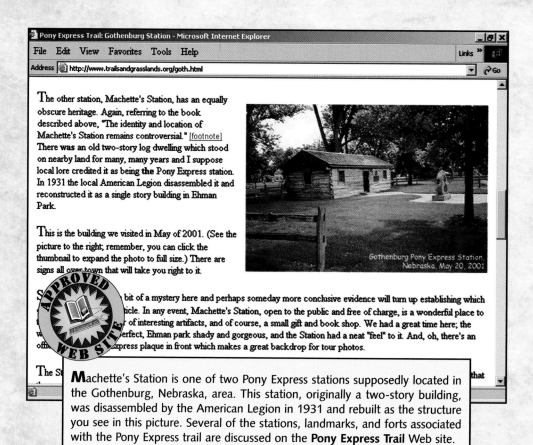

Pony Express Trail: Gothenburg Station - Microsoft Internet Explorer

File   Edit   View   Favorites   Tools   Help   Links

Address http://www.trailsandgrasslands.org/goth.html

The other station, Machette's Station, has an equally obscure heritage. Again, referring to the book described above, "The identity and location of Machette's Station remains controversial." [footnote] There was an old two-story log dwelling which stood on nearby land for many, many years and I suppose local lore credited it as being the Pony Express station. In 1931 the local American Legion disassembled it and reconstructed it as a single story building in Ehman Park.

This is the building we visited in May of 2001. (See the picture to the right; remember, you can click the thumbnail to expand the photo to full size.) There are signs all over town that will take you right to it.

Gothenburg Pony Express Station, Nebraska, May 20, 2001

... bit of a mystery here and perhaps someday more conclusive evidence will turn up establishing which ... icle. In any event, Machette's Station, open to the public and free of charge, is a wonderful place to ... of interesting artifacts, and of course, a small gift and book shop. We had a great time here; the ... erfect, Ehman park shady and gorgeous, and the Station had a neat "feel" to it. And, oh, there's an ... xpress plaque in front which makes a great backdrop for tour photos.

Machette's Station is one of two Pony Express stations supposedly located in the Gothenburg, Nebraska, area. This station, originally a two-story building, was disassembled by the American Legion in 1931 and rebuilt as the structure you see in this picture. Several of the stations, landmarks, and forts associated with the Pony Express trail are discussed on the **Pony Express Trail** Web site.

1,966-mile route. The main stations were adobe buildings or log cabins. They were staffed by stationmasters and stockkeepers. The larger stations provided food and bedding for horses and riders along with repair equipment and supplies. The smallest stations were nothing more than a man-made cave dug into a hillside or a tent pitched on flat land.

Each station had a corral and stalls for the horses. Altogether, there were between 150 and

190 relay stations located every 5 to 20 miles. Working at a station was a dangerous and lonely job. Although the workers were armed, they were often at the mercy of roaming bands of American Indians. Raids on stations were a common occurrence. It was not unusual for a rider to arrive at the station and find the workers killed and the livestock stolen.

The Riders' Equipment

Along with lightweight riders, the Pony Express used lightweight equipment to ensure speedy and timely delivery of the mail. The mail was carried in a four-pocketed leather pouch called a *mochila*. The mochila was designed to fit snugly over the saddle. Once it was in place, it completely covered the saddle and reached about halfway down to the stirrups. Three of the four pockets were padlocked, and the stationmaster was the only one with a key. The fourth pocket was used for mail picked up along the route.

The mochila was unattached and was held in place by the rider as he straddled the saddle. When the rider was changing horses, the mochila could be removed or slung over the saddle in a matter of seconds.

The saddle and bridle were also lighter than average. The mochila and saddle had a combined weight of 13 pounds. That was less than one third

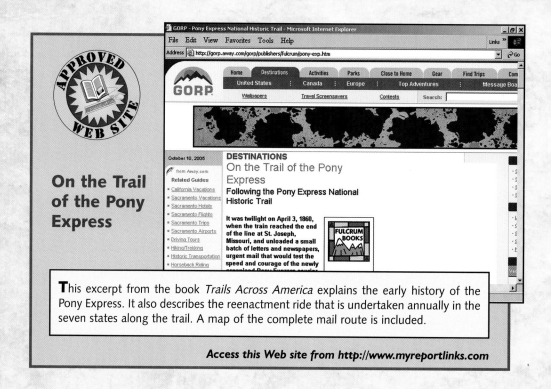

GORP – Pony Express National Historic Trail – Microsoft Internet Explorer

File   Edit   View   Favorites   Tools   Help   Links »

Address http://gorp.away.com/gorp/publishers/fulcrum/pony-exp.htm   Go

GORP

| Home | Destinations | Activities | Parks | Close to Home | Gear | Find Trips | Com |
| United States | | Canada | | Europe | | Top Adventures | | Message Boa |

Wallpapers   Travel Screensavers   Contests   Search:

On the Trail of the Pony Express

October 10, 2005

from Away.com

Related Guides
- California Vacations
- Sacramento Vacations
- Sacramento Hotels
- Sacramento Flights
- Sacramento Trips
- Sacramento Airports
- Driving Tours
- Hiking/Trekking
- Historic Transportation
- Horseback Riding

DESTINATIONS
On the Trail of the Pony Express
Following the Pony Express National Historic Trail

It was twilight on April 3, 1860, when the train reached the end of the line at St. Joseph, Missouri, and unloaded a small batch of letters and newspapers, urgent mail that would test the speed and courage of the newly

FULCRUM BOOKS

This excerpt from the book *Trails Across America* explains the early history of the Pony Express. It also describes the reenactment ride that is undertaken annually in the seven states along the trail. A map of the complete mail route is included.

Access this Web site from http://www.myreportlinks.com

of what a typical western saddle weighed. The maximum weight that a pony was allowed to carry was 165 pounds. That included the rider and 20 pounds of mail.

▷ Opening for Business

Most of the mail carried by the Pony Express was also light. It had to be, because they charged five dollars per half ounce. That cost was reduced a bit after a special lightweight paper was manufactured. Using the special paper, an eight-or ten-page letter could be mailed for around $2.50.

In early 1860, the Pony Express placed ads in newspapers announcing a new letter delivery service. Their ads proclaimed the upstart company would move a letter from New York City to San Francisco in only thirteen days. That included train time to the easternmost relay station in St. Joseph, Missouri.

Russell and his partners had agreed that the Pony Express would make its first run on April 3, 1860. As the day drew nearer, there was a mixture of excitement and cynicism. Many doubted that the new enterprise would be feasible. Russell, Majors, and Waddell looked forward to proving them wrong.

THE RIDERS' EXCITING RUNS

On March 30, 1860, the first mail for the Pony Express was put on trains in New York City and Washington, D.C. The destination was St. Joseph, Missouri. Unfortunately, a messenger delayed the first delivery by missing a train connection. When the messenger got on the awaiting mail train in Hannibal, Missouri, it was over two hours behind schedule.

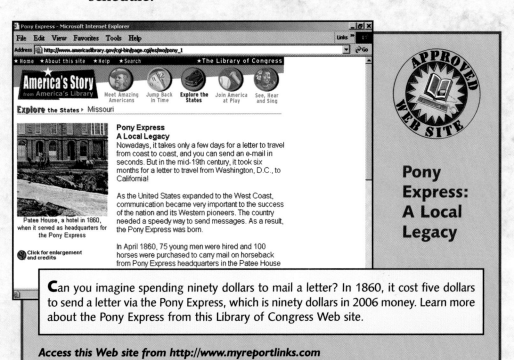

Pony Express - Microsoft Internet Explorer

File Edit View Favorites Tools Help   Links »

Address http://www.americaslibrary.gov/cgi-bin/page.cgi/es/mo/pony_1   Go

★Home ★About this site ★Help ★Search   ★The Library of Congress

America's Story from America's Library   Meet Amazing Americans   Jump Back in Time   Explore the States   Join America at Play   See, Hear and Sing

Explore the States ▶ Missouri

Patee House, a hotel in 1860, when it served as headquarters for the Pony Express

Click for enlargement and credits

Pony Express
A Local Legacy
Nowadays, it takes only a few days for a letter to travel from coast to coast, and you can send an e-mail in seconds. But in the mid-19th century, it took six months for a letter to travel from Washington, D.C., to California!

As the United States expanded to the West Coast, communication became very important to the success of the nation and its Western pioneers. The country needed a speedy way to send messages. As a result, the Pony Express was born.

In April 1860, 75 young men were hired and 100 horses were purchased to carry mail on horseback from Pony Express headquarters in the Patee House

Pony Express: A Local Legacy

APPROVED WEB SITE

Can you imagine spending ninety dollars to mail a letter? In 1860, it cost five dollars to send a letter via the Pony Express, which is ninety dollars in 2006 money. Learn more about the Pony Express from this Library of Congress Web site.

Access this Web site from http://www.myreportlinks.com

Things were in place to make up for lost time. The 206 miles of railroad track from Hannibal to St. Joseph had been cleared, and switches were closed to keep other trains off the track. As soon as the messenger stepped aboard, the engineer opened the throttle all the way. The powerful steam locomotive began speeding away.

At that time, a freight train would have a top speed of 15 miles per hour. Passenger trains were restricted to a top speed of 24 miles per hour. Faster speeds were considered too risky for the fragile track roadbeds. The speedy mail train covered the distance in four hours and fifty-one minutes. That averaged out to over 40 miles an hour. That would stand as a record speed for that route for fifty years.

The First Rider

In St. Joseph, an increasingly restless crowd watched the empty tracks. A brass band kept them entertained during the wait. The first rider sat astride a bay mare chosen to make the historic first run, but the rider had to return the horse to the stable.

While warming the horse up by leading her along the way, the fidgety crowd began swarming in on the mare. They began plucking hairs from her tail for souvenirs. The rider retreated to protect the horse from any further abuse.

The loud screech of the whistle alerted the crowd that the train was near. When it arrived, there was yet another delay. There was a round of speech making!

Former St. Joseph mayor M. Jeff Thompson predicted a bright future for the new enterprise and exhorted the crowd to give three cheers for the Pony Express. Majors then spoke and called the Pony Express a forerunner of "a more important and greater enterprise."[1] He predicted that a transcontinental railroad would one day open

http://www.legendsofamerica.com/photos-missouri/FirstRidePonyExpress-600.jpg - Microsoft Internet Explorer

File   Edit   View   Favorites   Tools   Help   Links »

Address   http://www.legendsofamerica.com/photos-missouri/FirstRidePonyExpress-600.jpg   Go

This painting by Charles Hargens, entitled *The First Ride,* depicts Pony Express rider Johnny Fry leaving the Pikes Peak Stables to go west, for the first time on April 3, 1860, at 7:15 P.M. He returned ten days later with the eastbound mail. This painting can be found online at the **Pony Express: Fasted Mail Across the West** Web page.

up vast expanses of western land to settlement. That railroad would eventually replace the Pony Express as the mail carrier linking the East and the West.

At around 7:15 P.M., Thompson placed the mochila over the saddle of the bay mare. The mochila contained forty-nine letters, five telegrams, and several copies of the *St. Joseph Daily Dispatch* newspaper. The first westward run of the Pony Express was over two hours late. The rider who took the mochila on its first trip west is still a matter of dispute. According to the Pony Express National Museum, Johnny Fry was the first westbound rider. Many historians believe that a rider named Johnson William Richardson was the first westbound rider, and that he won the honor in a drawing. Richardson definitely rode on the return trip.

Guaranteed Service

In newspaper ads placed in the spring of 1860, the Pony Express boldly said that it would deliver letters from San Francisco to New York in nine days. Letters going between San Francisco and Salt Lake City would be charged a rate of three dollars per half ounce. Letters going beyond Salt Lake City would cost five dollars per half ounce.

At those rates, letters were written on the thinnest, lightest paper possible. Usually, they were written on tissue paper, sealed into a tissue paper envelope and then placed in a pocket of oiled silk. The silk pocket protected the letters against water when a rider had to ford a stream or river.

Lightening the Load

The gear used by riders was also as lightweight as possible. For the first run, Fry (or Richardson) was armed with two Colt revolvers and a Spencer rifle. Later on, riders found that three guns were too much extra weight. They cut back to a single Colt revolver with an extra supply of ammunition.

The food they carried was sparse. The riders' pockets were filled with a few hard biscuits and some bacon strips. They also carried a small

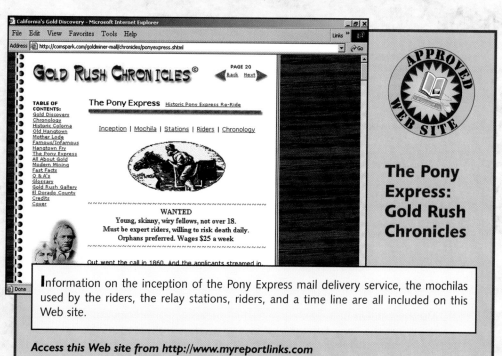

Information on the inception of the Pony Express mail delivery service, the mochilas used by the riders, the relay stations, riders, and a time line are all included on this Web site.

Access this Web site from http://www.myreportlinks.com

canteen filled with caffeine-laden tea to ward off drowsiness.

The saddle they used was called a Landis saddle, and it was favored for its durability and lightness. The saddle, blanket, and mail weighed a total of about forty pounds.

Completing the First Rides

Fry's first ride was a short one. It took him to a nearby ferry landing where a boat was waiting to transport him across the Missouri River to Elwood, Kansas. At Elwood, another crowd was waiting to

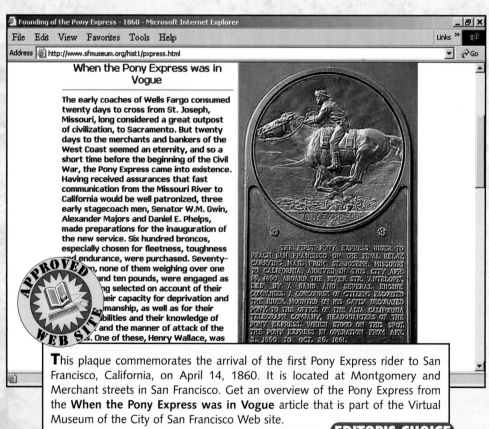

This plaque commemorates the arrival of the first Pony Express rider to San Francisco, California, on April 14, 1860. It is located at Montgomery and Merchant streets in San Francisco. Get an overview of the Pony Express from the **When the Pony Express was in Vogue** article that is part of the Virtual Museum of the City of San Francisco Web site.

EDITOR'S CHOICE

cheer him on. When he left Elwood, Fry was nearly two-and-a-half hours behind schedule.

Fry rode hard to make up for lost time. He changed horses three times and finished his run forty-five minutes ahead of schedule. The riders who followed him were not as fortunate. When the mochila reached Salt Lake City, it was over eighteen hours behind schedule. Rough, boggy trails, thunderstorms, and swollen streams all delayed the riders.

Making up for Lost Time

The start of the first eastbound run from San Francisco also had a festive air. There were brass bands playing, and fireworks lit up the sky. The pony was decorated with bells and miniature flags. The first eastern run began with a slight, comical miscue. James Randall was the first eastbound rider. In the excitement of the moment, Randall tried to mount his pony from the wrong side.

The crowd cheered when the embarrassed rider corrected his mistake. Then, Randall rode to the waterfront to place a mochila filled with eighty-five letters on a steamboat bound for Sacramento.

In Sacramento, rider Billy Hamilton was anxiously waiting for the mochila. His send-off was noticed only by a lone employee from the Express office. The steamboat *Antelope* finally docked in

Sacramento at around two o'clock in the morning. It was pitch-black and raining hard. Hamilton quickly took the mochila and began riding down a wet, dark trail. Hamilton found that many places in the road were flooded out. He called his 57-mile run "as black as the inside of a cow."[2] In spite of the darkness and the pelting rain, Hamilton finished his run thirty minutes ahead of schedule.

Hamilton was relieved by Warren Upson, for what may have been the most difficult part of the 1,966-mile route. Upson was ideally suited for making the difficult run. Although he was only twenty-one years old, he was already an experienced trapper, prospector, and woodsman. His ability to withstand and endure all kinds of adverse conditions gave him a reputation of being "weatherproof." Upson had a vast knowledge of mountain trails and passes.

Things That Impeded the Riders

Upson followed a twisting trail into the Sierra Nevada Mountains. While he rode along the steep and narrow route, rain turned to sleet and then to snow. The pony slowed down from a trot to a walk. The wintry weather had forced stagecoaches to cancel their trips through the mountain range. Upson gamely endured powdery, swirling snow and icy winds. Many times, he had to dismount and walk his pony.

A Pony Express rider leaving a relay station is depicted in "Coming and Going of the Pony Express" by Frederic Remington. Sometimes hazards of the trail stopped them from making their changes on time.

Extremely adverse weather was not the only obstacle that Upson faced. He had to abandon the regular trail because the path was blocked by a long procession of mule trains and freight wagons en route to mines in Nevada's Carson Valley. Upson avoided further delay by detouring through snowdrifts. There were frequent dismounts where Upson had to pull his horse through knee-deep and body-deep drifts.

Seven miles from the Friday's relay station on the California-Nevada border, Upson found his path blocked by an avalanche. He abandoned his pony and climbed a tall rock in search of a new route. By using his compass to guide him east and north, Upson made it to the Friday's Station.

When the trail began sloping downward, Upson realized that the worst was over. Around midnight, Upson reached Carson City, Nevada. After 85 grueling miles, the exhausted rider was ready to pass along the mochila to his eager replacement.

Beyond Carson City, there were 600 miles of icy and snowy ridges. Forty-seven relay stations placed 12 to 15 miles apart connected Carson City to Salt Lake City. To make up for lost time, the riders spurred their mounts to a full gallop. The eastbound mochila arrived in Salt Lake City 103

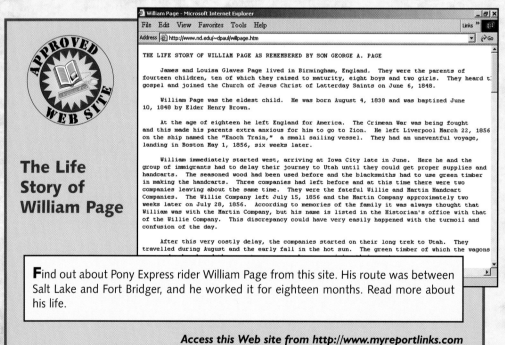

The Life Story of William Page

William Page - Microsoft Internet Explorer

File   Edit   View   Favorites   Tools   Help   Links »

Address http://www.nd.edu/~dpaul/willpage.htm   Go

THE LIFE STORY OF WILLIAM PAGE AS REMEMBERED BY SON GEORGE A. PAGE

   James and Louisa Glaves Page lived in Birmingham, England. They were the parents of fourteen children, ten of which they raised to maturity, eight boys and two girls. They heard t gospel and joined the Church of Jesus Christ of Latterday Saints on June 6, 1848.

   William Page was the eldest child. He was born August 4, 1838 and was baptized June 10, 1848 by Elder Henry Brown.

   At the age of eighteen he left England for America. The Crimean War was being fought and this made his parents extra anxious for him to go to Zion. He left Liverpool March 22, 1856 on the ship named the "Enoch Train," a small sailing vessel. They had an uneventful voyage, landing in Boston May 1, 1856, six weeks later.

   William immediately started west, arriving at Iowa City late in June. Here he and the group of immigrants had to delay their journey to Utah until they could get proper supplies and handcarts. The seasoned wood had been used before and the blacksmiths had to use green timber in making the handcarts. Three companies had left before and at this time there were two companies leaving about the same time. They were the fateful Willie and Martin Handcart Companies. The Willie Company left July 15, 1856 and the Martin Company approximately two weeks later on July 28, 1856. According to memories of the family it was always thought that William was with the Martin Company, but his name is listed in the Historian's office with that of the Willie Company. This discrepancy could have very easily happened with the turmoil and confusion of the day.

   After this very costly delay, the companies started on their long trek to Utah. They travelled during August and the early fall in the hot sun. The green timber of which the wagons

Find out about Pony Express rider William Page from this site. His route was between Salt Lake and Fort Bridger, and he worked it for eighteen months. Read more about his life.

Access this Web site from http://www.myreportlinks.com

hours and 45 minutes after leaving Sacramento. The route had been scheduled to take 110 hours.

The eastbound run was ahead of schedule, but the inaugural westbound run had failed to arrive on schedule. The St. Joseph-to-Salt Lake City route took 143 hours, which was around 18 hours late. The failure was blamed on a combination of swollen streams, stormy weather, and very muddy roads.

An Early Success

One on-time delivery and one late delivery was not the best start, but considering all the adverse conditions, it could have been worse. Nobody blamed the Pony Express for conditions that were beyond their control. They proved their point. This new system of man, horse, and relay stations could work.

The *San Francisco Daily Evening Bulletin* praised the early success of the Pony Express by writing: "California may be said to have been brought from ten to twelve days nearer to the rest of the civilized world."[3] The newspaper also noted that ocean mail that had left New York City on March 20 did not reach San Francisco until April 12.

But soon the Pony Express would be dealing with a more serious threat than bad weather. Much of their route ran through vast, unsettled expanses of native lands. In May 1860, the Paiute Indians would be on the warpath.

The Paiute War

During its short run, the Pony Express tried to avoid conflict and confrontation with American Indians. Unfortunately, that was not always possible. Two thirds of their route ran through hostile Indian country. The Indians looked upon the Pony Express stations and riders as trespassers.

It is not hard to understand why the American Indians felt that way. There is no record that the Pony Express ever purchased the land where their stations were built. The corridor used as the Pony Express route ran directly through Indian Territory. There is also no record that any part of that

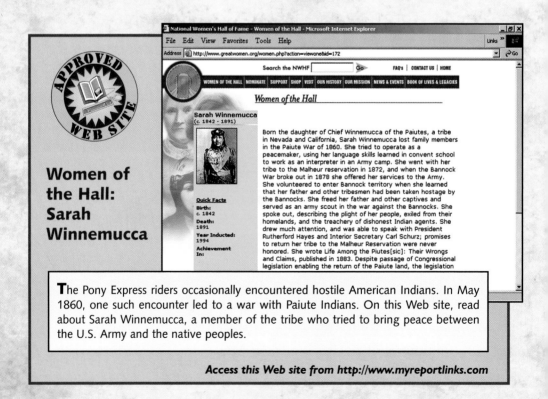

Women of the Hall: Sarah Winnemucca

National Women's Hall of Fame - Women of the Hall - Microsoft Internet Explorer

File Edit View Favorites Tools Help · Links »

Address http://www.greatwomen.org/women.php?action=viewone&id=172

Search the NWHF [ ] Go · FAQ's | CONTACT US | HOME

WOMEN OF THE HALL | NOMINATE | SUPPORT | SHOP | VISIT | OUR HISTORY | OUR MISSION | NEWS & EVENTS | BOOK OF LIVES & LEGACIES

Women of the Hall

Sarah Winnemucca
(c. 1842 - 1891)

Quick Facts
Birth:
c. 1842
Death:
1891
Year Inducted:
1994
Achievement
In:

Born the daughter of Chief Winnemucca of the Paiutes, a tribe in Nevada and California, Sarah Winnemucca lost family members in the Paiute War of 1860. She tried to operate as a peacemaker, using her language skills learned in convent school to work as an interpreter in an Army camp. She went with her tribe to the Malheur reservation in 1872, and when the Bannock War broke out in 1878 she offered her services to the Army. She volunteered to enter Bannock territory when she learned that her father and other tribesmen had been taken hostage by the Bannocks. She freed her father and other captives and served as an army scout in the war against the Bannocks. She spoke out, describing the plight of her people, exiled from their homelands, and the treachery of dishonest Indian agents. She drew much attention, and was able to speak with President Rutherford Hayes and Interior Secretary Carl Schurz; promises to return her tribe to the Malheur Reservation were never honored. She wrote Life Among the Piutes[sic]: Their Wrongs and Claims, published in 1883. Despite passage of Congressional legislation enabling the return of the Paiute land, the legislation

The Pony Express riders occasionally encountered hostile American Indians. In May 1860, one such encounter led to a war with Paiute Indians. On this Web site, read about Sarah Winnemucca, a member of the tribe who tried to bring peace between the U.S. Army and the native peoples.

Access this Web site from http://www.myreportlinks.com

territory was ceded to the Pony Express by any tribe or tribes.

Since the American Indians lived on that land long before the Pony Express arrived, they regarded it as their land. In desert areas, the Pony Express built their relay stations near watering holes. Water was a rare and precious resource. When the native people were deprived of that resource, conflict was inevitable.

Safety Tips

Pony Express riders were expected to observe a few general rules when encountering American Indians. They were:

If it is one Indian, be friendly.
If it is three Indians, be careful.
If it is ten Indians, run.
Never shoot first.

Riders were instructed to shoot low and keep shooting while avoiding unnecessary risks. They were reminded that the American Indians had rights since they were there first and the route was created on some of the lands that they still owned. They were further instructed to think of the mail first, the pony second, and their lives last.

The first recorded conflict between American Indians and the Pony Express was in mid-April 1860. The westbound run was delayed for six hours because American Indians drove off horses from the Roberts Creek station.

On May 7, 1860, an incident at the Williams Station in Nevada set off what became known as the Paiute War. The Williams Station was located about ten miles east of the Pony Express' Buckland's Station. It was a ranch founded and tended by three Williams brothers who had migrated from Maine.

▷ A Gruesome Discovery

When James O. Williams arrived at the station on May 8, he found that his brothers, Daniel and

△ *Some Pony Express relay stations and stables were in extremely isolated areas. Sometimes, a stationmaster did not know what he might find when he arrived. These Pony Express stables are in Fort Bridger, Wyoming.*

Oscar, had been murdered. Various accounts of the incident say that there were three to five other victims. Those accounts say that the bodies of the other victims were burned beyond recognition. Along with those victims, all the livestock had been driven off and all the structures had been burned to the ground.

Revenge?

Why the Williams brothers were killed is a matter of dispute. The likely reason was revenge for something the whites in the area had done. It is generally believed that some Paiute women were taken hostage and assaulted. Reportedly, one of the hostages' husbands tried to rescue them. After being rebuffed, he went for some reinforcements. He returned with about eight other Paiutes who helped him burn down the Williams Station.

When the Pony Express started, there was no open warfare with any tribe or tribes. In general, the Shoshone, the Pawnee, and the Kickapoo were friendly tribes. The Crow, the Cheyenne, and the Paiute were sometimes friendly and sometimes hostile.

Most of the time, Pony Express riders avoided trouble by outrunning and eluding hostile Indians. The horses the Indians rode were no match for the well-maintained and carefully chosen mounts of the Pony Express. It was safer and easier to run than it was to fight.

A Volunteer Army

The news of the attack on the Williams Station set off an all-out war between the settlers and the Paiute. Volunteers were organized into military units aimed at ridding the area of any American Indians they considered hostile. Most of the volunteers were ranchers and miners, but a few were professionally trained soldiers.

The best-known company of volunteers was led by Major William O. Ormsby. It was also the company that suffered the most casualties.

THE PERSUIT.

△ In this lithograph created by J. H. Bufford, a Pony Express rider is fleeing from raiding American Indians. Paiute Indians, especially, did not take kindly to the Pony Express riders crossing their native lands.

Ormsby's outfit was poorly armed and poorly trained, but that did not stop them from going after the Paiute.

After burying the victims at Williams Station, Ormsby's company of 105 men rode north to Pyramid Lake. Few of the men were experienced at fighting the American Indians, and it appears that they failed to scout the enemy.

On the afternoon of May 12, 1860, Ormsby led his company of men into a canyon a few miles south of Pyramid Lake. They were quickly and easily ambushed by the awaiting enemy. The Paiute were aided by some Shoshone and Bannock warriors. They killed seventy-six of Ormsby's men and wounded twenty-nine more.

The few survivors quickly retreated and were pursued for about 15 to 20 miles. Major Ormsby was killed when he tried to surrender.

In late May 1860, a force of about 750 volunteers and United States soldiers went after the Paiute. They chased them across Nevada and reportedly killed about 160 Paiute and members of other tribes in several different skirmishes.

▶ Attacks Go On

That was not enough to stop the American Indian raids. Pony Express stations in Nevada and Utah still fell under attack. Station workers and riders were killed in the sporadic attacks. An unofficial total claimed that seven stations were destroyed, sixteen employees were killed, and about 150 horses were driven off.

The attacks forced the Pony Express to temporarily suspend service just as it was getting started. Different estimates say that service was stopped for three weeks to two months. The total cost to the Pony Express was an estimated seventy-five thousand dollars. Courier service had to be reestablished, the routes resecured, and stations had to be rebuilt and restocked with horses, supplies, and workers. New stations were built with 8-foot-high stone walls protecting the structure.

After resuming operations, an uneasy peace with the Paiute was often broken. Skirmishes continued almost as long as the Express stayed in business. But even when the American Indian troubles were minimized, the financial troubles never went away. That, and the completion of the telegraph line, are what would ultimately doom the Pony Express.

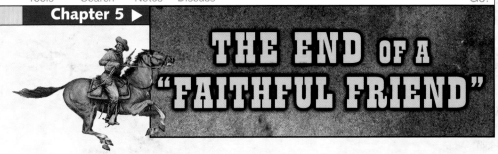

THE END OF A "FAITHFUL FRIEND"

In spite of much favorable publicity, the Pony Express continued to lose money at an alarming rate. There were estimates that the new enterprise was losing one thousand dollars a day. The Pony Express was a subsidiary of a company named the Central Overland, California & Pike's Peak Express. A joke began going around that the initials COC&PP stood for Clean Out of Cash and Poor Pay.

Hoping to increase business, they continually lowered their rates. In August 1860, the rate for a half-ounce letter was lowered from $5 to $2.50. In April 1861, they reduced the rate to two dollars. On July 1, 1861, the rates were lowered to only one dollar. While lowering rates, the Pony Express was spending about sixteen dollars for every letter it delivered.

▶ A Money Loser

The rate cuts never brought in enough new business to make up for the reductions in revenue. Their outgo continued to exceed their income. The

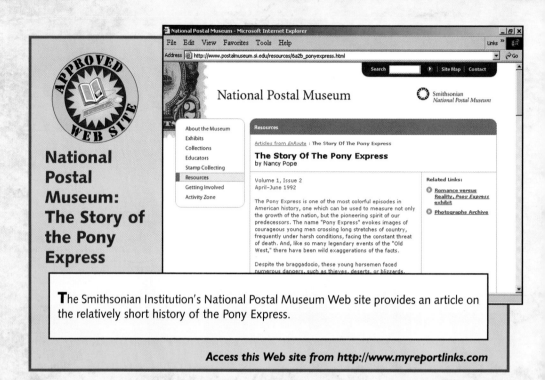

National Postal Museum: The Story of the Pony Express

The Smithsonian Institution's National Postal Museum Web site provides an article on the relatively short history of the Pony Express.

Access this Web site from http://www.myreportlinks.com

Pony Express might have survived longer if the freighting business of Russell, Majors, and Waddell had been doing well. Unfortunately, they were also having financial problems.

Their freighting business was also losing money because they had been underbid on an important Army contract. They were still getting business from the Army, but the Army was slow in providing them with delivery instructions. While awaiting the Army's instructions, they had to pay workers for being idle.

With a downturn in business, Russell, Majors, and Waddell were finding it harder to get loans and credit. Although they were able to continue to

Secretary of War John B. Floyd served in President Buchanan's Cabinet.

meet the Pony Express payroll, workers for their freighting firm and stagecoach line were some-times going unpaid.

William Russell was often spending more and more time trying to raise money. In the summer and fall of 1860, he kept calling on Secretary of War John Floyd for unpaid, past-due payments for their Army freighting services. Russell did manage to get a partial payment of $161,000, but that did not begin to cover the large debts his firm had incurred.

Impressive Feats

In an effort to boost business, the Pony Express used the results of the 1860 presidential election to show its speed and efficiency. On November 7, 1860, a rider left Fort Kearney, Nebraska, with the news of Abraham Lincoln's election. In spite of a heavy snowstorm, the news reached Salt Lake City in only three days and four hours. From Salt Lake City, the news was carried to the telegraph station at Fort Churchill, Nevada. News of Lincoln's election reached California newspapers on November 14. It was an impressive feat, but sadly, it did not improve business.

Shortly after Lincoln was inaugurated in March 1861, the Pony Express made the fastest westward run in its history. By that time, seven states had seceded from the Union to form the Confederate

To try to attract more business, the Pony Express did a publicity stunt in which they got the results of the Election of 1860 to the West Coast in just over three days. It failed to drum up business. The election was won by Abraham Lincoln.

States of America (CSA). The Civil War between the North and South was unavoidable. People in the West were very eager to read what Lincoln had to say about the impending war.

There were concerns that California would support the Confederacy instead of the Union. Lincoln's Inaugural Address had to reach Sacramento in the shortest possible time. Knowing this, Russell, Majors, and Waddell had made elaborate advance plans to speedily send Lincoln's speech westward. They hired hundreds of extra workers for the special project. Arrangements were made to have fresh relay horses ready every 10 miles between St. Joseph and Sacramento. Only seven days and seventeen hours after Lincoln's Inaugural Address was telegraphed from Washington, D.C., to Saint Joseph, it was received in Sacramento.

A Bad, Desperate Decision

Once, the Pony Express was sued for failing to pay a debt. A company that provided equipment and feed to stations got tired of going unpaid. As a result, the court ordered the Pony Express to settle the debt by giving the company all of its livestock in Utah.

A public outcry by the residents of Salt Lake City pressured the unpaid firm to drop the matter. The loss of livestock would have caused Utah to be cut off from the Express' coast-to-coast mail service.

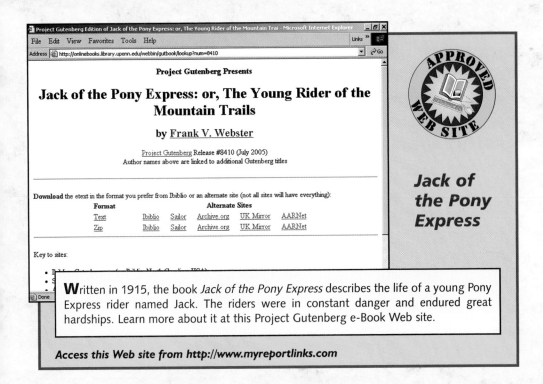

Jack of the Pony Express

Written in 1915, the book *Jack of the Pony Express* describes the life of a young Pony Express rider named Jack. The riders were in constant danger and endured great hardships. Learn more about it at this Project Gutenberg e-Book Web site.

Access this Web site from http://www.myreportlinks.com

The constant financial problems and the threat of an impending bankruptcy finally caused Russell to act foolishly. Russell told a friendly banker named Luke Lea that his businesses were in deep financial trouble. Lea told Russell that Goodard Bailey, a law clerk in the Department of the Interior, might be able to help him out.

Bailey had control of bonds that were being held in a trust to help out various American Indian tribes. Bailey and Russell hatched a scheme. Russell would "borrow" some bonds from Bailey and use them as collateral for obtaining bank loans. When the loans were repaid, Russell would return the bonds to Bailey.

Russell signed some credit vouchers for Bailey to hold. That way, if the missing bonds were discovered, Bailey had proof that the intent was to borrow, not steal, the bonds. In December 1860, bonds with a total value of $870,000 were found to be missing. This was balanced out by $870,000 worth of credit vouchers signed by Russell.

On Christmas Eve 1860, Russell was arrested and charged with three counts of receiving stolen property and one count of conspiring to defraud the government. After spending a few days in jail, Russell was released on a three-hundred-thousand-dollar bond.

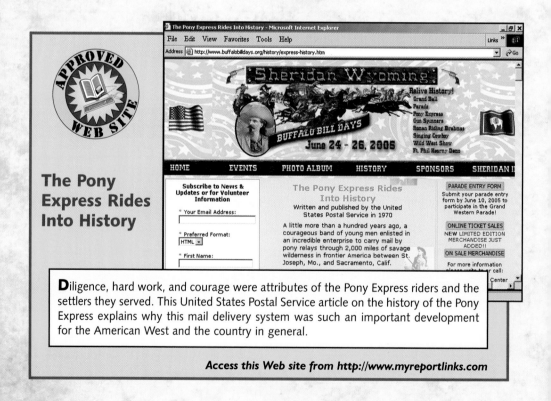

The Pony Express Rides Into History

Diligence, hard work, and courage were attributes of the Pony Express riders and the settlers they served. This United States Postal Service article on the history of the Pony Express explains why this mail delivery system was such an important development for the American West and the country in general.

Access this Web site from http://www.myreportlinks.com

In January 1861, members of the U.S. House of Representatives established a committee to investigate Russell and Bailey's scheme. Russell testified four times. Sometimes, he was evasive; other times he was forthright. Often, he seemed confused when trying to recall exact dates and precise sums of money. Although he was briefly imprisoned, Bailey was able to avoid testifying.

Also in January 1861, Russell was brought to trial in the Criminal Court in Washington, D.C. Thanks to the work of his clever defense attorney, Russell was able to avoid being convicted. The attorney cited an 1857 law that said anyone who had testified before a congressional committee could not be prosecuted for crimes involved in their testimony. The case against William Russell was dismissed.

A New Mail Route for a Competitor

While Russell was testifying in court and before the select congressional committee, Congress was debating a new mail contract. The Pony Express had shown that a central mail route could work and that it was more feasible than the longer southern route. In February 1861, the House passed a bill calling for daily mail service using a central route. If the bill had passed the Senate, it could have kept the Pony Express in business a while longer.

As the bill was being debated in the Senate, Confederate forces cut off the southern mail route. The Butterfield Overland Mail Company had been using the southern route. The bill was amended to require Butterfield to move their operations to the central mail route. The amendment also put an end to competitive bidding for the mail contract.

Bankrupt

After the bond scandal occurred, few members of Congress cared about the financial problems of the Pony Express. They were not about to trust Russell with a million-dollar mail contract. The firm of Russell, Majors, and Waddell went into bankruptcy.

Yet, Russell found a way to keep the company afloat. The bankrupt firm still had assets such as relay stations, livestock, stagecoaches, and trained workers that Butterfield needed. In March 1861, Russell agreed to give up the western half of the central route to Butterfield. In exchange, Butterfield agreed to share the lucrative mail contract with the Pony Express. The Overland Mail Company now controlled the deliveries between Salt Lake City and Sacramento.

The Last Run

Russell's triumph was short-lived. Their creditors wanted him removed, and the board of directors

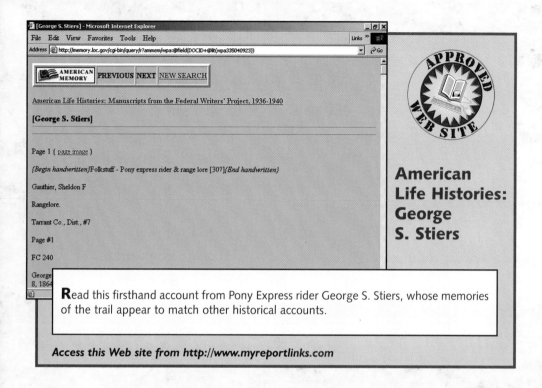

[George S. Stiers] - Microsoft Internet Explorer

File Edit View Favorites Tools Help   Links »

Address 🔳 http://memory.loc.gov/cgi-bin/query/r?ammem/wpa:@field(DOCID+@lit(wpa335040923))   ▼ 🔗 Go

AMERICAN MEMORY **PREVIOUS NEXT** NEW SEARCH

American Life Histories: Manuscripts from the Federal Writers' Project, 1936-1940

[George S. Stiers]

Page 1 (page image)

{Begin handwritten}Folkstuff - Pony express rider & range lore [30?]{End handwritten}

Gauthier, Sheldon F

Rangelore.

Tarrant Co., Dist., #7

Page #1

FC 240

George
8, 1864

American Life Histories: George S. Stiers

Read this firsthand account from Pony Express rider George S. Stiers, whose memories of the trail appear to match other historical accounts.

Access this Web site from http://www.myreportlinks.com

forced Russell to resign on April 26, 1861. The Pony Express managed to live on for a few more months. On November 21, 1861, the last rider completed the last run.

The passing of the Pony Express was noted by many newspapers. The *California Pacific* mourned the loss by writing: "A fast and faithful friend has the Pony been to our far-off state. Summer and winter, storm and shine, day and night, he has traveled like a weaver's Shuttle back and forth till now his work is done. Goodbye, Pony! . . . We have looked to you as those who wait for the morning, and how seldom did you fail us! . . . You have served us well!"[1]

▶ Invention of the Telegraph

It has been written that nothing on wheels could kill the Pony Express; its death came through the air. For most of its history, the Pony Express carried mail and messages between areas unconnected to the telegraph. When the country became completely wired, the Pony Express was no longer needed.

In 1859, the California Legislature pledged six thousand dollars a year to subsidize construction of a telegraph line connecting them with the East Coast. A year later, Congress voted to pay forty thousand dollars a year for ten years to any company that could erect a telegraph line from the

The First Transcontinental Telegraph System Was Completed

Fast delivery was, and still is, one of the most important aspects in the delivery of mail. The Pony Express was fast but could not compete with a transcontinental telegraph system. Use the "next" button to follow along with this Library of Congress article.

Access this Web site from http://www.myreportlinks.com

middle western to the far western states. The states in the East already had a network of telegraph lines and services. In the Far West, Los Angeles and San Francisco were connected by wire and lines extended eastward into Nevada.

Following the Pony Express Route

James Gamble and Edward Creighton are the two men who receive most of the credit for the completion of the transcontinental telegraph. Gamble worked on extending the lines eastward from the Sierra Nevadas. Creighton worked on the route that followed the trail established by the Pony Express.

For such a massive project, construction of the lines went pretty smoothly. Gamble and Creighton organized the project by dividing the workforce into four crews. One crew surveyed the land and laid out the line, another crew installed the poles, a third crew strung the wires, and the fourth crew set up the work camps and fed the workers.

There was interference from American Indians, but it did little to slow down construction. The most resistance came from the Paiute, who would shoot at the wires as they were being strung. Builders told the various tribes that the wires were "bad medicine" and interference with them would anger the air spirits.

This painting by George M. Ottinger shows a Pony Express rider galloping past men constructing a telegraph line. The telegraph lines followed the path of the Pony Express and were partially responsible for putting it out of business.

The visible presence of armed Pony Express riders riding past the wires and poles also helped to keep American Indians from interfering with the project. Ironically, these riders were helping protect a project that would hasten their demise.

On October 24, 1861, the western and eastern sections of the transcontinental telegraph were linked at Salt Lake City, Utah. The project was completed on time and under budget. Two days later, the Pony Express officially ceased daily operations, although it would make some scattered deliveries until November 1861.

Life After the Pony Express

The end of the Pony Express was also the end of the business careers of Russell, Majors, and Waddell.

William Russell returned to New York City and began working as a stockbroker. He was not able to make a living as a stockbroker, so he turned to doing any work he could find. Bankers and financiers who once courted his business now avoided and rebuffed him. He lived in a succession of cheap boardinghouses until his family rescued him. He was living with his son, John, when he died in 1872.

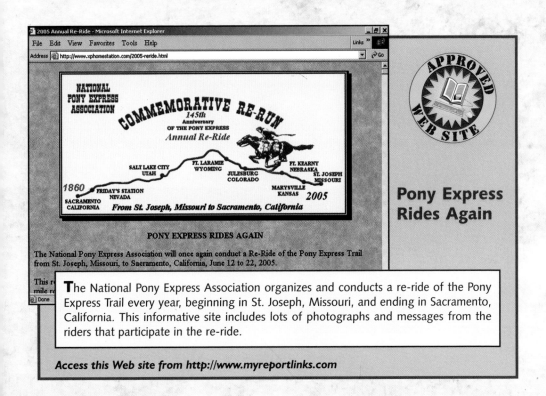

Pony Express Rides Again

The National Pony Express Association organizes and conducts a re-ride of the Pony Express Trail every year, beginning in St. Joseph, Missouri, and ending in Sacramento, California. This informative site includes lots of photographs and messages from the riders that participate in the re-ride.

Access this Web site from http://www.myreportlinks.com

△ This plaque appears on a marker at one of the Pony Express stations in Gothenburg, Nebraska. The engraving shows the images of Pony Express founders Russell, Majors, and Waddell.

William Waddell never worked again. He returned to his home in Lexington, Missouri. His last years were dreary and stressful. He was repeatedly sued by angry creditors and old friends who had turned against him. Land that he owned was sold when he could not pay his taxes. He was living with his daughter when he died at age sixty.

Alexander Majors returned to a life of hard labor. He ran some small freighting businesses and graded roadbeds for the Union Pacific Railroad. For a time, he tried working as a prospector. He was living in a small mining shack outside of Denver when his former employee, Buffalo Bill Cody, became reunited with him.

Majors was writing his autobiography, and Cody helped him out by paying to get it edited and printed. Majors died in Chicago in 1900 when he was eighty-six.

Chapter 6 ▶

FAMOUS FEATS AND RIDERS

William F. "Buffalo Bill" Cody was one of the most famous figures of the Wild West to be associated with the Pony Express. Cody was renown for his deeds as an American Indian scout and fighter, and as a buffalo hunter. There are numerous tales about Cody's Pony Express adventures, but the length and exact nature of his employment with the company is a matter of dispute.

▶ Legendary Stories

Different sources give Cody's year of birth as 1845 or 1846. That means Cody would have been only fourteen or fifteen years old when he rode for the Pony Express. That is not as unlikely as it sounds. In the 1860s, America had no laws restricting children from working full-time jobs.

Historians and researchers have combed through the records of the Pony Express and compiled a list of about 120 riders. The name William F. Cody appears several times in those records.

It is an undisputed fact that Cody worked for Alexander Majors. Majors hired him in 1857 to

This was the ranch owned by Buffalo Bill Cody. It is located in North Platte, Nebraska.

work as a messenger between wagon trains en route to Utah. Cody was paid twenty-five dollars a month.

Many of the stories about Cody's adventures with the Pony Express were created by a writer named Ned Buntline. Buntline knew Cody and briefly spent some time with him. It resulted in a book entitled *Buffalo Bill: The King of the Border Men—The Wildest and Truest Story I Ever Wrote.* Buntline was probably right when he said it was the wildest story he ever wrote. However, he was probably wrong when he said it was the truest. In his autobiography, Cody wrote that he rode for the Pony Express for two years. However, the Pony Express was only in business for about nineteen months.

Whether it is fact or fiction, Cody is credited with making the longest ride in the Pony Express' brief history. According to Majors, Cody rode the

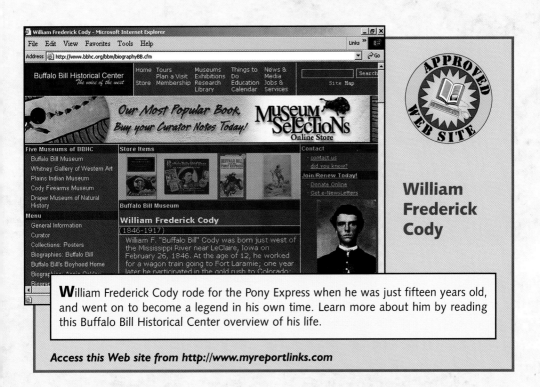

William Frederick Cody rode for the Pony Express when he was just fifteen years old, and went on to become a legend in his own time. Learn more about him by reading this Buffalo Bill Historical Center overview of his life.

Access this Web site from http://www.myreportlinks.com

116-mile route between Red Buttes Station in Wyoming and the Three Crossings Station in Nebraska. Majors claims that one time Cody rode into Three Crossings and discovered that his replacement rider had been killed. Cody agreed to make an extra run until a replacement rider could be found. It is claimed that Cody rode a total of 384 miles and was on or ahead of schedule the whole time.

Amazing Bravery

Another story is that Cody once thwarted an attempted robbery by carrying an extra mochila stuffed with papers. Two bandits ambushed Cody in a narrow pass and threatened to kill him if he did not surrender the mochila. Cody threw the extra mochila in one robber's face and then shot him in the shoulder. Cody then escaped by remounting his pony and outrunning the second robber.

In their book *Saddles and Spurs,* Raymond W. Settle and Mary Lund Settle write about how hard it is to separate fact from fiction.

Numerous stories are told of young Cody's adventures as a Pony Express rider, but how many of them are true, and how many are pure fiction concocted by such writers as Ned Buntline will never be known. The same is true concerning his own writings in later years when his fame had become

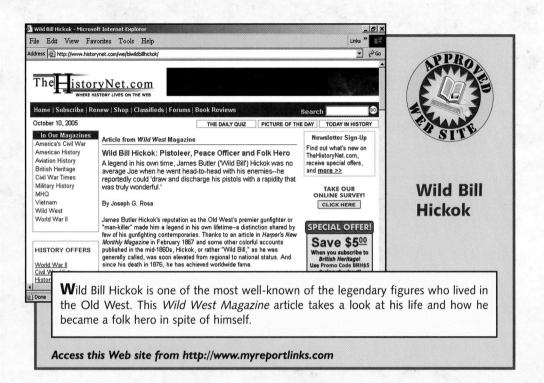

Wild Bill Hickok - Microsoft Internet Explorer

File   Edit   View   Favorites   Tools   Help   Links »

Address 🔗 http://www.historynet.com/we/blwildbillhickok/   ⭐ Go

The HistoryNet.com
WHERE HISTORY LIVES ON THE WEB

Home | Subscribe | Renew | Shop | Classifieds | Forums | Book Reviews   Search _____ GO

October 10, 2005   THE DAILY QUIZ   PICTURE OF THE DAY   TODAY IN HISTORY

In Our Magazines
America's Civil War
American History
Aviation History
British Heritage
Civil War Times
Military History
MHQ
Vietnam
Wild West
World War II

HISTORY OFFERS

World War II
Civil War History
History

Article from *Wild West* Magazine

Wild Bill Hickok: Pistoleer, Peace Officer and Folk Hero
A legend in his own time, James Butler ('Wild Bill') Hickok was no
average Joe when he went head-to-head with his enemies--he
reportedly could 'draw and discharge his pistols with a rapidity that
was truly wonderful.'

By Joseph G. Rosa

James Butler Hickok's reputation as the Old West's premier gunfighter or
"man-killer" made him a legend in his own lifetime--a distinction shared by
few of his gunfighting contemporaries. Thanks to an article in *Harper's New
Monthly Magazine* in February 1867 and some other colorful accounts
published in the mid-1860s, Hickok, or rather "Wild Bill," as he was
generally called, was soon elevated from regional to national status. And
since his death in 1876, he has achieved worldwide fame.

Newsletter Sign-Up
Find out what's new on
TheHistoryNet.com,
receive special offers,
and **more >>**

TAKE OUR
ONLINE SURVEY!
CLICK HERE

SPECIAL OFFER!
Save $5⁰⁰
When you subscribe to
British Heritage!
Use Promo Code BRH$5

Done

Wild Bill Hickok is one of the most well-known of the legendary figures who lived in the Old West. This *Wild West Magazine* article takes a look at his life and how he became a folk hero in spite of himself.

Access this Web site from http://www.myreportlinks.com

Wild Bill
Hickok

APPROVED WEB SITE

worldwide. Certain it is that in both cases imagination was allowed considerable freedom.[1]

▶ Wild Bill Hickok

Another famous western figure associated with the Pony Express is the lawman and gunfighter, James Butler "Wild Bill" Hickok. Hickok was never a rider, but he did work as a stock tender at the Pony Express station in Rock Creek, Nebraska.

While working for the Pony Express, Hickok was in a confrontation where he killed one man and wounded another. The gunfight helped to establish Hickok's reputation as a gunslinger.

Hickok's victim was a man named David McCanles. McCanles had a reputation for being a bully and brute. He also had a history or teasing and tormenting the usually docile Hickok.

McCanles was upset because the firm of Russell, Majors, and Waddell owed him money for hay and unpaid rental fees. McCanles had made repeated attempts to collect the debt. Whenever he tried to collect, he was told that the money was on its way.

On July 12, 1861, McCanles made yet another trip to the Rock Creek Station to demand payment on the long overdue debt. McCanles was accompanied by his cousin, James Woods; his son, Monroe; and their neighbor, James Gordon. All four of them were unarmed.

▶ Deadly Confrontation

McCanles went to the cabin where the station-master, Horace Wellman, lived. Woods, Gordon, and Monroe waited for McCanles at the station's barn. McCanles knocked on the front door and Mrs. Wellman answered. She told McCanles that her husband was inside, but he would not come outside. McCanles would not tolerate Wellman's cowardice. He told Mrs. Wellman: "send him out or I'll come in and drag him out."[2]

Hickok was inside the cabin when he overheard McCanles threaten Wellman. While Wellman

In July 1861, Wild Bill Hickok and David McCanles were involved in a deadly disagreement at the Rock Creek Station. Rock Creek was an important stop on the Oregon Trail and the Pony Express.

cowered inside the cabin, Hickok walked to the doorway and began talking to McCanles. McCanles insisted that the dispute was none of Hickok's business. Then he told Hickok: "All right, if you want to take a hand in this, come out and we'll settle it like men."[3]

Hickok knew that a no-holds-barred, fair fight with David McCanles was out of the question. He also knew that he had had enough of being bullied by McCanles. He stood safely in the doorway and refused to step outside. Once again, David McCanles threatened to come into the station after Wellman, if they would not send him outside.

McCanles decided that he would wait no longer. He stepped inside the cabin. Wild Bill Hickok stopped McCanles with a single shot from a

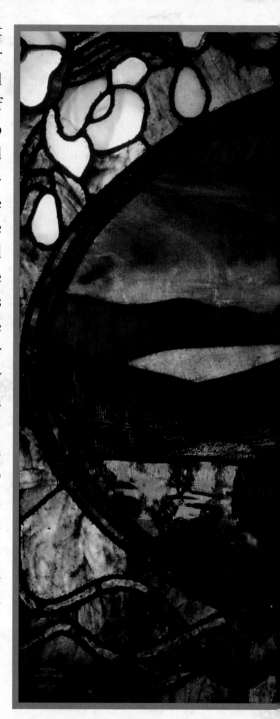

This stained glass image of a Pony Express rider can be found at the Rock Creek Station. Rock Creek was a popular place for the riders to change horses.

Hawkins rifle. The fatal bullet struck McCanles in the heart. Ironically, the rifle Hickok used was given to Wellman by McCanles for self-defense.

When Woods and Gordon heard the shot, they ran toward the cabin. Hickok began firing at them with a Colt revolver. One account says that Hickok fired twice and missed both men. Another account says that Woods was wounded. Both accounts agree that Woods and Gordon began fleeing for their lives.

Wellman chased down Gordon and killed him by hitting him in the head with a hoe. Woods was chased down by Wellman and a stock tender named Doc Brink. Brink killed Woods with a single blast from a shotgun. While Gordon and James Woods were being chased and killed, Monroe held his father and watched him die.

Self-Defense?

Monroe Woods was able to escape and report the killings to the authorities. Hickok, Wellman, and Brink were arrested on July 15. They appeared before Justice of the Peace T. M. Coulter. The accused trio pleaded self-defense and further argued that they were protecting government property because on the premises there were wagons, horses, and stages used to carry the United States mail. Justice Coulter agreed and freed all three of the men without even holding a trial.

▵ Most Pony Express riders were relieved and glad to see one another at the relay stations. On the right, you can see the mochila changing hands as it goes from one mount to the next.

In an 1867 interview, Hickok claimed that McCanles entered the cabin with a gun aimed at him. He further claimed that McCanles was the ringleader of an outlaw gang. Hickok also made an outlandish claim that he killed eleven men in the ensuing skirmish while suffering thirteen stab wounds and eleven buckshot wounds.

The tall tales told by Hickok helped him get hired as the town marshal in Abilene, Kansas. A lawless man was able to become the law in a lawless town.

Captain Jack Slade

Hickok was not the only Pony Express employee to live outside the law. Joseph Alfred "Captain Jack" Slade was another notable example. Sometimes, you had to use an outlaw to stop an outlaw. That is what the Pony Express did when they assigned Slade to clean up their operations.

By his thirteenth birthday, Slade had already earned a reputation for having an uncontrollable temper. When a man began bothering Slade and some of his school friends, Slade killed him by striking him in the head with a rock. Sources claim that Slade killed between twenty and twenty-six people before a lynch mob ended his life.

Slade was originally hired to supervise the construction of about two hundred Pony Express relay stations. He was also responsible for tending to their stable of horses and hiring drivers. It is believed that Slade hired Buffalo Bill Cody when Cody was just fifteen years old.

▷ Jules Reni

The Pony Express was having many problems in a 200-mile stretch of territory from Julesburg, Colorado, to eastern Wyoming. The operations in that area were supervised by Jules Reni, who was a bully and an outlaw. The settlement of Julesburg had been named for Reni. It was truly his town. Reni would brag that he was the law in Julesburg.

Reni used his position to give outlaws advance information on the movements of the mail and stagecoach lines.

After Captain Jack Slade replaced Reni as an area superintendent, Reni ambushed and shot Slade. Reni thought that he had killed Slade, but he was sadly mistaken. Slade recovered from his wounds and formed a posse to hunt down Reni.

Reni was captured and brought to Slade. Slade took his revenge by coldly and methodically murdering Reni. He lashed Reni to a corral post and let him stand there overnight. The following morning, Slade used Reni as a human target.

Between shots, Slade gulped whiskey and sadistically told Reni where the next gunshot was going. Reni was shot twenty-two times before Slade put down his pistol. Then, Slade cut the ears

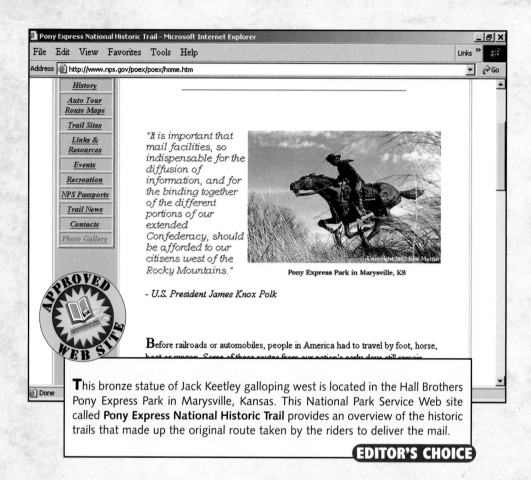

"It is important that mail facilities, so indispensable for the diffusion of information, and for the binding together of the different portions of our extended Confederacy, should be afforded to our citizens west of the Rocky Mountains."

- *U.S. President James Knox Polk*

Before railroads or automobiles, people in America had to travel by foot, horse,

This bronze statue of Jack Keetley galloping west is located in the Hall Brothers Pony Express Park in Marysville, Kansas. This National Park Service Web site called **Pony Express National Historic Trail** provides an overview of the historic trails that made up the original route taken by the riders to deliver the mail.

EDITOR'S CHOICE

off of Reni's lifeless body. One account says that Slade carried them with him as souvenirs. Another story says that Slade nailed them to the door of the Julesburg Station.

Tales of Bravery and Endurance

The behavior of Hickok and Slade was not typical of the brave riders of the Pony Express who routinely risked their lives and sacrificed their safety to carry the mail. In the short history of the Pony

Express, there are numerous tales of valor and heroism.

▷ Jack Keetley

Jack Keetley rode for the Pony Express during the entire nineteen months they were in business. He made the longest continuous ride in the history of the Pony Express. Since they were short on riders, Keetley rode for thirty-one hours without dismounting. He covered 340 miles before being relieved. For most of the last five hours, Keetley slept in the saddle.

"It was all right as long as I didn't fall off," Keetley said. "The pony knows the route as well as I do."[4]

▷ Nick Wilson

Nick Wilson was a rider who used his wits and his rapport with American Indians to save his life. Wilson ran away from his Mormon home in Grantsville, Utah, when he was nine years old. For two years, he lived as a member of the Shoshone Chief Washakie's family. He learned their language and their ways.

When he was fifteen, Wilson was hired as a rider. Once he found himself in a narrow gorge with four American Indians blocking his path. Wilson tried to turn back, but there were three more tribesmen blocking his escape route. He was

This Pony Express reenactment rider is alone with his horse. Most of the time, Pony Express riders were by their lonesome. Sometimes, though, the riders had unwanted company in the form of American Indian raiders who sought to chase the Pony Express from their lands.

at their mercy. All he could do was wait to see what they were going to do.

Fortunately, Wilson knew one of the American Indians. He was a warrior named Tabby whom he had known when he lived with his parents in Grantsville. A one-eyed American Indian who was the leader of the band used a ramrod to mark a trail in the road. The leader announced: "We will burn stations here and here, and we will kill the Pony men."[5]

http://www.webpanda.com/white_pine_county/historical_society/images/CountyPlaces/ruby_ponyx_sta - Microsoft Interne...

File   Edit   View   Favorites   Tools   Help   Links »

Address   http://www.webpanda.com/white_pine_county/historical_society/images/CountyPlaces/ruby_ponyx_station.jpg   Go

Done

"Uncle Billy" Rogers established a trading post at Ruby Valley, located in Nevada, in 1859. One year later, the Pony Express built a station there. This picture of the Ruby Valley Pony Express Station was taken in 1944. Read about other area stations at the **Pony Express Stations in White Pine County, Nevada,** Web site.

The warriors gathered together to talk amongst themselves. After they built a fire, Wilson gave them all the tobacco he had with him as a peace offering and gesture of friendship. Tabby began talking to Wilson and told him that the other warriors wanted to kill him, but he would not go along with it because Wilson's father was his friend. Wilson had to promise them that he would never again carry the mail through the area.

Wilson Makes a Deal

Wilson feared for his life, but he told Tabby that this time the mail he carried had to go through. As a compromise, he promised that he would never ride through that area again. Wilson kept his promise by transferring to another route. It is not known what happened to the rider or riders who took over Wilson's old route.

On another occasion, Wilson pursued two American Indians who had stolen horses from the Antelope Station. He chased them into a cedar grove and was shot in the head by a man firing a flint-tipped arrow.

A couple of station employees tried to remove the arrow, but the shaft broke. The flint-tipped arrowhead remained lodged in Wilson's head. The two employees assumed that Wilson was dying, so they rolled him under a tree and took off for the next station.

The next morning, they returned to bury Wilson. To their amazement, Wilson was still breathing. They carried him to Cedar Wells and sent a rider to Ruby Valley to fetch a doctor. When the doctor arrived, he removed the arrowhead and instructed them to keep a wet rag over the wound. Reportedly, Wilson was unconscious for over three weeks.

Somehow he recovered and returned to work. For the rest of his life, Wilson wore a hat to cover the scar.

Station Keepers and Stock Tenders

While the dauntless riders of the Pony Express got most of the attention and the glory, the station keepers and stock tenders who manned the relay stations have often gone unnoticed. They were truly the unsung heroes of the Pony Express.

Working at a relay station was a lonely job. The riders who dashed in and out twice a week seldom had time for any polite conversation. Often, the only time they could converse with someone from the outside world was when a teamster would drive in the monthly supply wagon from the home station.

It was also a dangerous and dirty job. They had to be constantly on the lookout for hostile American Indians and hope that their rifles and ration of ammunition could repel an attack. The

▲ *Many of the Pony Express relay stations were just primitive outposts. This woman holds up a newspaper article announcing the creation of the Pony Express. She is a reenactor at the station in Gothenburg, Nebraska.*

scarcity of water during certain times of the year made it impossible for them to bathe, shave, or wash their clothes and blankets. Their garments and bedding would become infested with lice. The only solution was to lay their clothes and blankets over an anthill and let the ants eat the lice.

The food they ate was bland, plain, and sometimes in short supply. The main staples of their diet were bacon, beans, dried fruit, cornmeal, and coffee. While their food might run low, there was always plenty of grain and hay for the horses.

Some station names suggest what stark, drab places they were: Muddy Creek, Sand Hill, Lone Tree, and Dry Creek to name a few. As one went farther west on the trail, the stations became even more primitive and crude. One traveler described the Dugway Station in Utah as "a hole, four feet deep, roofed over with split cedar trunks, and with a rough adobe chimney. Water had to be brought in casks."[6]

▷ Jealousy and Conflict

Living in isolated areas with little outside contact caused station employees to lash out at each other. Even though they signed a pledge not to quarrel or fight with other employees, it was not always possible to obey it.

Once, a spat between a station keeper and a rider led to a murder. A rider named Montgomery

Maze was on a westbound run when he stopped at the Smith's Creek Station. For some reason, the station keeper, H. Trumbo, did not have a fresh mount ready to go. Maze used foul and abusive language to tell Trumbo what he thought of him. Trumbo responded by pulling out his pistol.

Trumbo aimed and pulled the trigger, but the gun was not loaded. Trumbo was probably aware it was not, but Maze did not know. Maze was not going to brush off a death threat. The next day, when he retraced his route to go east, Montgomery Maze was armed.

Without a word of warning, Maze shot Trumbo with a rifle. Trumbo died, and Maze was later arrested and charged with murder. Maze had two stock tenders sign a statement that Trumbo threatened his life. On the basis of their testimony, Maze went free.

The murder of Trumbo was an isolated incident. For the most part, the men of the Pony Express were dedicated and hardworking.

Chapter 7 ▶

LEGACY OF A DARING ENTERPRISE

The Pony Express was short-lived, but long remembered. In nineteen months, it delivered over thirty-four thousand pieces of mail and helped to lay the groundwork for coast-to-coast communication and transportation in a young, rapidly growing nation.

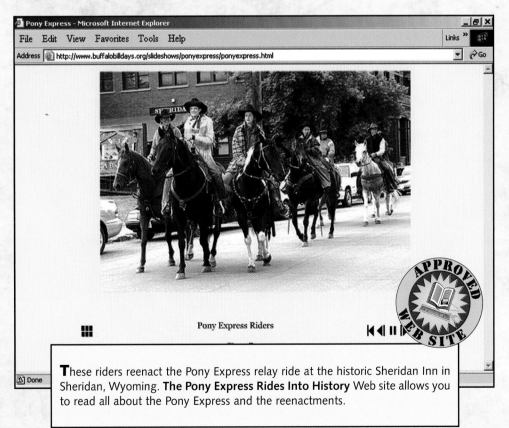

Pony Express - Microsoft Internet Explorer

File   Edit   View   Favorites   Tools   Help   Links »

Address http://www.buffalobilldays.org/slideshows/ponyexpress/ponyexpress.html   Go

Pony Express Riders

These riders reenact the Pony Express relay ride at the historic Sheridan Inn in Sheridan, Wyoming. **The Pony Express Rides Into History** Web site allows you to read all about the Pony Express and the reenactments.

▲ The Pony Express helped to keep California in the Union during the hectic time prior to the Civil War. This was despite the efforts of some such as General Albert Sidney Johnston.

The daring enterprise was a financial failure. The business never made a profit. Its founders and backers lost over two hundred thousand dollars. Some estimates place the losses as high as seven hundred thousand dollars. A government mail contract perhaps would have made the business briefly profitable, but the advent of the telegraph and the Transcontinental Railroad still would have made the Pony Express obsolete.

Accomplishments

Historians credit the Pony Express with two main accomplishments. It proved that the central route was the best route for delivering mail from the East Coast to the West Coast. The central route would be the route chosen for connecting the country by telegraph and later by railroad. Eight years after the Pony Express ceased operations, the eastern and western United States were linked by the Transcontinental Railroad.

The second major accomplishment was keeping California in the Union when the Southern states were seceding to form the Confederate States of America. There was a genuine threat that California would side with the Confederacy. There were many Californians who were openly sympathetic to the Confederacy and wanted California to secede.

An image of the Pony Express station at the jumping off point of St. Joseph, Missouri. This building is now part of The Pony Express National Museum.

Albert Sidney Johnston

The most prominent Californian with Southern sympathies was Army General Albert Sidney Johnston. General Johnston was a close friend of Confederate States of America President Jefferson Davis. When the Confederacy was being formed, Johnston was serving in California commanding the U.S. Army's Department of the Pacific.

Different historians offer different opinions of Johnston. Some historians say that Johnston was loyal to the Union and kept the proslavery and Confederate sympathizers in California from open rebellion. A more commonly held view is that Johnston was plotting with Senator Gwin to turn California over to the Confederacy. Reputedly, there was a cache of over one hundred thousand guns stashed away in warehouses and ranches from Los Angeles to Seattle.

A Union loyalist named Edmund Randolf told James McClatchey that Johnston was ready to turn over all the weapons in a Benicia, California, arsenal to the Confederacy. McClatchey used the Pony Express to rush a secret message to President Lincoln. Lincoln replaced Johnston with General Edwin Vose Sumner, whose loyalty to the Union was unquestioned.

There is no disputing which side Johnston took once the Civil War began. After Texas seceded from the Union, Johnston sided with the

Confederacy. He served the CSA as a general and commanded all the Confederate troops west of the Allegheny Mountains before being mortally wounded at the Battle of Shiloh.

Senator Gwin also left California to join the Confederacy. After the war, he fled to Mexico before finally returning to California.

The Stories Live On

Over 140 years after its demise, the Pony Express still remains alive in the hearts and minds of historians and writers who chronicled the winning of

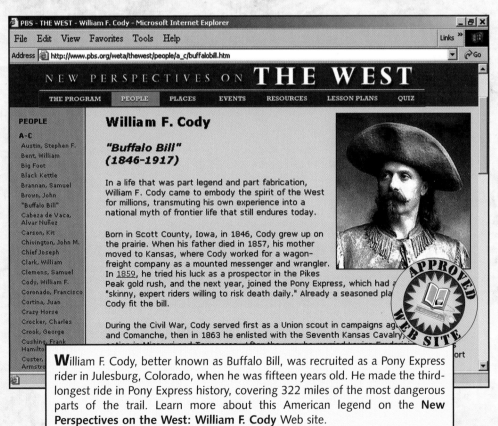

PBS - THE WEST - William F. Cody - Microsoft Internet Explorer

File   Edit   View   Favorites   Tools   Help   Links »

Address http://www.pbs.org/weta/thewest/people/a_c/buffalobill.htm   Go

NEW PERSPECTIVES ON THE WEST

THE PROGRAM   PEOPLE   PLACES   EVENTS   RESOURCES   LESSON PLANS   QUIZ

PEOPLE

A–C
Austin, Stephen F.
Bent, William
Big Foot
Black Kettle
Brannan, Samuel
Brown, John
"Buffalo Bill"
Cabeza de Vaca, Alvar Nuñez
Carson, Kit
Chivington, John M.
Chief Joseph
Clark, William
Clemens, Samuel
Cody, William F.
Coronado, Francisco
Cortina, Juan
Crazy Horse
Crocker, Charles
Crook, George
Cushing, Frank Hamilton
Custer, Armstrong

William F. Cody

"Buffalo Bill"
(1846–1917)

In a life that was part legend and part fabrication, William F. Cody came to embody the spirit of the West for millions, transmuting his own experience into a national myth of frontier life that still endures today.

Born in Scott County, Iowa, in 1846, Cody grew up on the prairie. When his father died in 1857, his mother moved to Kansas, where Cody worked for a wagon-freight company as a mounted messenger and wrangler. In 1859, he tried his luck as a prospector in the Pikes Peak gold rush, and the next year, joined the Pony Express, which had "skinny, expert riders willing to risk death daily." Already a seasoned pl[a] Cody fit the bill.

During the Civil War, Cody served first as a Union scout in campaigns ag[ainst] and Comanche, then in 1863 he enlisted with the Seventh Kansas Cavalry,

APPROVED WEB SITE

William F. Cody, better known as Buffalo Bill, was recruited as a Pony Express rider in Julesburg, Colorado, when he was fifteen years old. He made the third-longest ride in Pony Express history, covering 322 miles of the most dangerous parts of the trail. Learn more about this American legend on the **New Perspectives on the West: William F. Cody** Web site.

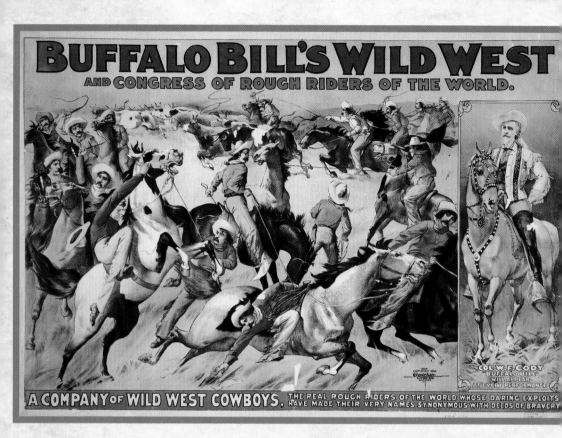

An advertisement for Buffalo Bill's famous Wild West Show depicts the story of the Pony Express. This part of the show grew in popularity as a result of its place in the show.

the West. Buffalo Bill Cody's Wild West Show glorified its short run. Since then, writers of western fiction and moviemakers continue to exalt the enterprise. Although the line separating fact and fiction, and truth from legend, has become blurred, there remains much to admire.

A trio of risk-taking businessmen put their careers on the line in the hope of reaping great rewards. They recruited a band of brave men to deliver mail and maintain relay stations in hostile territory. With little regard for their personal safety and comfort, loyal workers dedicated themselves to the difficult task of moving mail across rivers, deserts, mountains, and plains in sweltering heat and chilling blizzards.

That was the reality and the glory of the Pony Express.

Report Links

The Internet sites described below can be accessed at http://www.myreportlinks.com

▶**Pony Express National Historic Trail**
Editor's Choice Learn about the Pony Express routes and trails on this Web site.

▶**The Pony Express National Museum**
Editor's Choice Visit the virtual home of this important museum.

▶**Map of the Pony Express Route**
Editor's Choice Take a look at the Pony Express route.

▶**Pony Express Riders**
Editor's Choice A list of Pony Express riders is available on this site.

▶**When the Pony Express Was in Vogue**
Editor's Choice This is an early summary of the Pony Express.

▶**History of the U.S. Postal Service 1775–1993**
Editor's Choice Learn the history of mail service in the United States from this site.

▶**American Life Histories: George S. Stiers**
The Library of Congress presents an interview with former Pony Express rider George S. Stiers.

▶**The First Transcontinental Telegraph System Was Completed**
When you visit this Web page, you will find out how the telegraph affected the Pony Express.

▶*Harper's Weekly Illustrated Magazine:* **The Overland Pony Express**
Read this article on the Pony Express from an 1867 issue of *Harper's Weekly.*

▶**Historian Finds Pony Express Ad**
The missing newspaper advertisement is finally found!

▶**The History**
A short summary of the Pony Express can be read on this site.

▶**How the West Was Written**
Read the story of communication in the early days of the United States.

▶*Jack of the Pony Express*
Full-text online version of a book about the Pony Express is available here.

▶**The Life Story of William Page**
A biography of a Pony Express rider.

▶**National Postal Museum: The Story of the Pony Express**
Read about the history of the Pony Express from the National Postal Museum.

Report Links

The Internet sites described below can be accessed at http://www.myreportlinks.com

▶**New Perspectives on the West: William F. Cody**
A biography of William F. Cody, also known as Buffalo Bill.

▶**On the Trail of the Pony Express**
At this site, follow the Pony Express National Historic Trail.

▶**The Pony Express**
Photographs, information, the first telegraph message, and much more can be found on this site.

▶**The Pony Express: Gold Rush Chronicles**
Here is a good outline of the Pony Express.

▶**Pony Express: A Local Legacy**
Read a short overview of the Pony Express.

▶**Pony Express: Fasted Mail Across the West**
Here is a fact-filled information site on the Pony Express.

▶**Pony Express History**
This is a portal of very good Pony Express information.

▶**Pony Express Rides Again**
Visit this site for information on the annual Pony Express reenactment ride.

▶**The Pony Express Rides Into History**
Browse this excellent article on the history of the Pony Express.

▶**Pony Express Stations in White Pine County, Nevada**
Here is a history of the White Pine County, Nevada, Pony Express relay stations.

▶**Pony Express Trail**
The trails of the Pony Express are spotlighted here.

▶**Pushing the Envelope**
This *Smithsonian Magazine* article gives a history of envelopes.

▶**Wild Bill Hickok**
You can read a biography of Wild Bill Hickok on this Web site.

▶**William Frederick Cody**
The life and times of Buffalo Bill Cody are covered on this Web site.

▶**Women of the Hall: Sarah Winnemucca**
Winnemucca was a Paiute Indian. They attacked riders who encroached on their land.

adobe building—A building made out of heavy, sun-dried clay and straw.

alkali bottoms—Low-lying arid soil found in deserts.

bunkhouse—An easy-to-build structure that gave a group of people a place to sleep.

collateral—Assets pledged by a borrower to secure a loan or other credit.

contractor—One who works on a contract basis usually to construct or repair buildings.

conveyance—A vehicle or tool used to transport something.

credit voucher—A certificate exchangeable for cash.

farrier—One who shoes horses or gives them medical treatment.

forty-niner—A person who traveled west to take part in the Gold Rush. Named for 1849, the year that most people looked to strike it rich in California.

general store—A store that is usually located in a rural area and carries a wide array of items.

isthmus—A slender piece of land that connects two much larger landmasses.

meander—To follow a winding or turning path rather than a straight line.

mochila—A lightweight, four-pocketed mail pouch used by Pony Express riders.

outfit—The act of supplying or providing equipment for a voyage or journey.

Paiute—American Indian people who originally lived in the areas that are now Utah, Arizona, California, and Nevada.

polygamy—The practice of having more than one wife or husband at a time.

provisions—Supplies or materials needed to complete a journey or project.

relay station—A structure along the Pony Express route that would supply rest and relief to riders as they passed along their mochila to the man who was assigned to complete the next leg of the run.

sink—A large hole or opening in the ground that usually would fill with water.

station keeper—*See* stationmaster.

stationmaster—A person in charge of a Pony Express relay station.

teamster—A person who drives a team of horses or oxen.

thoroughbreds—Horses of pure breeding that are known for being light and quick.

trust fund—Property or money held in a trust.

Chapter 1. "Pony Bob's" Dangerous Ride

1. Christopher Corbett, *Orphans Preferred: The Twisted Truth and Lasting Legend of the Pony Express* (New York: Broadway Books, 2003), p. 192.

2. Kate B. Carter, *Riders of the Pony Express* (Salt Lake City, Utah: Pony Express Memorial Commission of Utah, 1952), p. 22.

3. Ibid.

4. Tom West, *Heroes on Horseback* (New York: Four Winds Press, 1969), p. 18.

5. Ibid.

6. Ibid., p.19.

7. Corbett, p. 193.

8. Ibid., p. 194.

Chapter 2. Mail Routes to the West

1. Anthony Godfrey, Ph.D., "By Ocean Or By Land: Roots of the Pony Express," *Pony Express National Historic Trail: Historic Research Study*, August 1994, <http://www.nps.gov/poex/hrs/hrs1.htm> (September 22, 2005).

2. Richard D. Poll, "The Utah War," *Utah History Encyclopedia*, n.d., <http://www.media.utah.edu/UHE/index_frame.html> (September 22, 2005).

Chapter 3. Starting Up the Business

1. Tom West, *Heroes on Horseback* (New York: Four Winds Press, 1969), p. 142.

2. Anthony Godfrey, Ph.D., "The Great Race Against Time: Birth of the Pony Express," *Pony Express National Historic Trail: Historic Research*

Study, 1994, <http://www.nps.gov/poex/hrs/hrs2b.htm> (September 22, 2005).

3. Ibid.

4. Samuel Hopkins Adams, *The Pony Express* (New York: Random House, 1950), p. 31.

5. Christopher Corbett, *Orphans Preferred: The Twisted Truth and Lasting Legend of the Pony Express* (New York: Broadway Books, 2003), p. 85.

Chapter 4. The Riders' Exciting Runs

1. Raymond W. Settle and Mary Lund Settle, *Saddles and Spurs: The Pony Express Saga* (Lincoln: University of Nebraska Press, 1955), p. 57.

2. Tom West, *Heroes on Horseback* (New York: Four Winds Press, 1969), p. 53.

3. Christopher Corbett, *Orphans Preferred: The Twisted Truth and Lasting Legend of the Pony Express* (New York: Broadway Books, 2003), p. 59.

Chapter 5. The End of a "Faithful Friend"

1. David Nevin, *The Expressmen* (New York: Time-Life Books, 1974), p. 113.

Chapter 6. Famous Feats and Riders

1. Raymond W. Settle and Mary Lund Settle, *Saddles and Spurs: The Pony Express Saga* (Lincoln: The University of Nebraska Press, 1955), p. 83.

2. Richard O'Connor, *Wild Bill Hickok* (New York: Ace Books, 1959), p. 16.

3. Ibid.

4. Samuel Hopkins Adams, *The Pony Express* (New York: Random House, 1950), p. 120.

5. Robert West Howard, *Hoofbeats of Destiny* (New York: Signet Books, 1960), p. 102.

6. Tom West, *Heroes on Horseback* (New York: Four Winds Press, 1969), p. 108.

Brill, Marlene Targ. *Bronco Charlie and the Pony Express.* Minneapolis, Minn.: Carolrhoda Books, Inc., 2004.

DiCerto, Joseph, J. *The Saga of the Pony Express.* Missoula, Mont.: Mountain Press Publishing Co., 2002.

Harness, Cheryl. *They're Off!: The Story of the Pony Express.* New York: Simon & Schuster Books for Young Readers, 1996.

Kroll, Steven. *Pony Express!* New York: Scholastic, 1996.

McCormick, Anita Louise. *The Pony Express in American History.* Berkeley Heights, N.J.: Enslow Publishers, Inc., 2001.

Moeller, Bill, and Jan. *The Pony Express: A Photographic History.* Missoula, Mont.: Mountain Press Publishing Co., 2003.

Payment, Simone. *The Pony Express: A Primary Source History of the Race to Bring Mail to the American West.* New York: Rosen Central Primary Source, 2005.

Rau, Margaret. *The Mail Must Go Through: The Story of the Pony Express.* Greensboro, N.C.: Morgan Reynolds Publishing, 2005.

Riddle, John. *The Pony Express.* Broomhall, Pa.: Mason Crest Publishers, 2003.

Stevenson, Angela. *Buffalo Bill: Frontier Daredevil.* New York: Aladdin Books, 1991.

Williams, Jean Kinney. *Pony Express.* Minneapolis, Minn.: Compass Point Books, 2003.